Money. People are happy when they have it and unhappy when they don't. And more and more people seem to have less and less money. In his book Alan explains why many people don't have enough money. And he gives many practical suggestions on how people can make more money and keep more of the money they make.

This is no ordinary book about money. This book won't just give you sound advice. It will give you the biblical and historical principles of money management as the source of that sound advice.

I highly recommend this book. But don't just read it. Share it with your children and grandchildren and neighbors and friends and business associates. This is a highly transformative book and one you will find difficult to put down. I hope it is a blessing to you as it has been to me.

—Steve Speichinger, Pastor
First Community Church
Hebron, NE

Alan is a talented writer, who brings together both the spiritual as well as the practical application of money management, in an understandable way that demonstrates both the causes and the cures for the creation of a solid and secure debt free retirement. Imagine for a moment following a plan, step-by-step, that will progress you to a point where you are not only in control of your finances, but you can now see clearly what your retirement years will look like. So take the money worries out of your mind by reading this book, and follow Alan's system. I highly recommend, *Managing Your Money Spiritually (Secrets of the Ages Revealed)!*

—Dr. Joel Tetreau, B.A., M.A., M.Div., D.Min.

MANAGING YOUR MONEY SPIRITUALLY!

(Secrets of the Ages Revealed)

ALAN W. HAYDEN

ISBN: 978-1-944878-58-0

CONTENTS

*This book is dedicated to my son,
Steven Hayden, an honest man,
a dependable Christian man.*

*Wisdom has to do with becoming skillful in honoring our parents
and raising our children, managing our money, going to work
and exercising leadership, using words well and treating friends
kindly, eating and drinking healthily, and cultivating emotions
and attitudes towards others that make for peace. We should be
maximizing God, and minimizing ourselves, by keeping connected
in holy obedience to the ordinary. After all, God is the potter, we
are the clay!*

INTRODUCTION

Many books have been written on the subject of personal money management, which is understandable considering the poor financial state of many American households. Therefore, it is clearly a subject very much in demand. I have found, however, that in doing my research I have discovered two groups of authors who write on this topic. There are Christian writers who emphasize the spiritual side of money management, but provide no practical, every day solutions to real world financial problems. The other group comprises professional money management authors who provide practical and useful information that can be implemented in solving modern day financial challenges, but they provide no spiritual approach to how God expects us to manage our money. This book, therefore, makes a valiant attempt to marry the two approaches, so that you can use the free services of God to act as your partner. Why would you need God as your partner? The answer is that He knows the future, do you? By using the biblical principles mentioned in this book, you will be able to move forward with a plan to bring your money management challenges under control, and work with a proven approach, grounded in real world money solutions, that will provide you with a financially worry free retirement, while at the same time pleasing All Mighty God with the way you live your life.

It is amazing to me that politicians, business men, and bankers, are always complaining about the ignorance the general public has about money, yet they have done a very poor job of doing anything about it. American society, in general, expects its citizens to take full responsibility for the management of their own income and expenses, and expects them to purchase a home rather than rent. Society also leaves it in the hands of individuals to charter their own road-map for a worry-free retirement, and to make their own decisions regarding health insurance (although a recent attempt has been made to change this). Sadly, as you will soon see, many citizens are seriously missing the mark. Many surveys demonstrate, as you will learn in a later chapter, that 4 out of 10 do not pay-off their credit card balances each month; 29% don't know what interest rate they are paying; 30% claim their interest rate is below 10%; 50% of high school students state they learned very little about money and finances; 61% do not know how compound interest rates work, and 59% do not know the difference between a company pension, social security, or a 401K retirement plan. Yet, these same students are being released into society, and expected to somehow survive. If this is not a prescription for a life of poverty I don't know what is.

Today in America, millions of people, old and young, married and single, college students, and even some high school kids, are gasping for air under heavy loads of debt that will take many years to repay. In fact it is fair to say that the majority of American households are being weighed down by debts that are strangling their freedom, and causing sleepless nights, stress, angst, worry about their futures, and especially not being able to one day enjoy a secure and dignified retirement. Married couples end up being separated or even divorced over money matters, which rocks the very foundation of the family unit, the glue that holds our society together. Many people live in dreaded fear of losing their home, their wheels, or being cut-off from credit access all together. Some even lose their jobs over debt issues.

We generally don't kick a man when he's down, but in the big world of the American credit industry, when people end up with a poor credit rating, they are taken advantage of with interest rate increases. Some people have such poor credit they can't even borrow from a check-cashing operation. But since times millennium there has always been the loan shark ready to prey on the poorest of the poor. I have known poor people being charged 25% interest per week on small loans. They don't understand that this rate amounts to 11 million percent per year! Shakespeare once said that we are all ignorant, only on different things. Clearly, a lack of money management skills is at the heart of such problems.

Even though the United Nations has outlawed slavery around the world, we find that debt creates a form of pernicious slavery that, if it gets out of control, can throw your life into chaos if you stop paying attention to fundamentals, and take the wrong attitude towards money management. Debt can also seriously inhibit your retirement plans, and no one wants to be working during their retirement years just to pay debt, and experience an impoverished lifestyle.

Let me provide you with a quick illustration of how easy it is to get further and further in debt if you don't think hard and long about how you spend your money before you actually spend it:

> Jeff and Linda Chavez came home from work tired one Friday night, and decided to have a pizza delivered. They rationalized the purchase on the basis that it was cheaper that eating out. But the $15.00 pizza was charged on their credit card, which already had an outstanding balance of $5,000.00, thus taking the balance to $5,015.00. They had traditionally been paying the minimum monthly payment of $100.00 (2% of the balance), with an interest charge of 20%. What they did not realize was that the pizza, which would have cost them $15.00 if they had paid cash, would in actual fact eventually cost them more than double the price due to the power of compound interest charges. Furthermore, they also failed to comprehend the fact that it would take almost a decade to pay-off the credit card in full, and they would pay $10,800.00 in total payments according to bankrate.com! This, of course, assumes they do not charge anything else on the card until the balance is paid in full, which is unlikely. Would Jeff and Linda have been willing to pay $30.00 for the pizza? I doubt it. Jeff and Linda are obviously unaware of these facts, and that is just the way the banks want it, to keep this couple in ignorance so the profits keep piling up. This story also illustrates the minimum payment affliction, which is becoming pervasive in many households. Talk to any car salesman who will tell you that their customers pay more attention to what the monthly payment will be, rather than what the total cost of the car is going to be.

By reading this book, and faithfully following the principles of spiritual money management, that I describe, which are biblical principles written down thousands of years ago, you will not only get out of debt, but put a plan in place that will mathematically improve your chances of prosperity and enjoying a solid retirement. But you must act now rather than later, because time and compound interest calculations wait for no one. The longer you put off executing an action plan, the more it will cost you down the road. In fact, many of you will find that by the time you have read this book, the interest you owe on one of your credit cards will be much greater than the cost of this book! I will even go one-step further by stating if the contents of my book do not literally save you thousands of dollars, and earn you much more on your investments, then I will fully refund your money! So act now! Read this book from beginning to end, and in the second read, start your plan of action to secure your future.

Managing a household that is free from debt, or debt that is low and manageable, allows you to breathe and prosper. Instead of worrying about how the bills are going to get paid, you can spend more time figuring out the best investments, and planning for your future. You will have peace of mind, which is something which we cannot put a dollar value on, but is a beautiful thing nonetheless. Listen to what St. Paul says in Philippians 4:7, "… and the peace of God, which transcends all understanding, will guard your hearts and minds in Jesus Christ." Many people have restless hearts that yearn to have more and more, over what they already have, but find no contentment because it is never enough. It's like people who eat too much. It's not what they eat, but what is "eating" them!

Here again, St. Paul says this: "I am not saying this because I am in need, for I have learned to be content whatever the circumstances. I know what it is to be in need, and I know what it is to have plenty. I have learned the secret of being content in any and every situation, whether well fed or hungry, whether living in plenty or in want. I can do everything through him who gives me strength." (Philippians 4:11).

FAILURE IS NOT AN OPTION!

Let me state right at the beginning that we are going to defeat the debt monster in your life, and we will put together a life-long plan to enable you to enjoy a worry free retirement. Failure is not an option! We will get the job done, but I am not saying it will be easy. You will need to discipline your mind to follow through on all the action points that I mention – no short-cuts! The steps are easily explained, but if you do not follow through, then you are demonstrating a lack of seriousness about your own retirement. Make the effort, and you will be well rewarded.

We all know how easy it is to become negative, especially when we are being hounded by creditors, or we are between jobs. No matter how bad your debt situation appears, it is always best to have an action plan, to be bold, and to face the problems rather than running away from them. Why am I so confident that you will succeed? It's simple. I'm going to ask you to start putting God first in your life, especially regarding all things financial. You will gain a better understanding of why this is so very important a little later in the book.

I am a big picture type of guy who is always looking to put matters into proper perspective. So, before we start addressing micro household financial issues, let us first look at the bigger macro economy in order to gain more wisdom and understanding in how we have come to manage our own household budget the way we do. This perspective, I believe, is a healthy exercise in helping us better understand how households get into so much debt in the first place.

America is drowning in a self-inflicted sea of debt that is unprecedented in the annals of history. Who can imagine government sovereign debt approaching $20 trillion! To put this figure into some type of perspective, try to imagine our federal government attempting to reduce this debt by writing checks in the amount of $1 million dollars every hour of every day going back to the time of Jesus Christ walking the earth, and there would still be more checks to write! Perhaps the last dime would be paid when Alexander the Great broke the Gordian Knot in the third century B.C! Pay no mind to the fact that our country is only 240 years old! This figure works out to about $311,000.00 per American household. To make matters even worse, we have sold out our future by incurring unfunded liabilities (these are obligations that must be paid in the future for pensions and other obligations, even though cash reserves have not been set aside to pay for them when they come due) in the amount of some $127 trillion! This amounts to $1.1 million per tax payer according to Forbes Magazine (1.17.14). No doubt the figures continue to rise.

At the consumer level, which accounts for about 70% of American private spending, we have incurred financial obligations that, in some cases, may never be paid back during the lifetime of the borrower. According to nerdwallet.com, at the end of 2016, home mortgage debt exceeded $8 trillion. Automobile debt is now well over $1 trillion; personal credit card debt is a whopping $938 billion, and student loans are an incredible $1.31 trillion! Since 2003, household income has increased 28%, whereas medical expenses have risen 57%, food and beverage costs are up 36%, and housing costs are up 32%. Incomes are clearly not keeping up with the cost of living.

These type of debt numbers per household would have our grandparents turning over in their graves! Banks are making obscene profits by aiding and abetting Americans in encouraging them to charge more and more, thus making the banks' lucrative credit card divisions the highest and best profit centers in the banking industry. We discuss this subject in greater scope in a later chapter.

As daunting as the above numbers are, America still has a great opportunity to turn this debt spiral around, because we have the power to change it due to our control of the world's largest reserve currency (explained later). Not only can our federal government eventually pay off this huge debt, so can every American pay off their debt that faithfully follow the action plan in this book.

Unfortunately, basic money management skills are not currently being given the priority they deserve in our public school systems, and consequently many kids have no idea of the importance of personal money management. This book, however, is a great start in that by teaching parents a successful money management plan, they can begin teaching their own children so the next generation does not repeat the debt game that has been going on now for the last 50 plus years.

Also, since 1963, we have stopped teaching the laws of God in our public school system, and therefore our kids are not aware of the fact that money management principles are mentioned more than 2,000 times in the Bible. Using the Law of Proportionality, it becomes obvious that God has a great deal to say about money, and the proper stewardship we should apply when managing it.

Today, we have avaricious credit companies inundating our young with credit card applications even before they graduate from high school, even though they are clueless on how to balance a check book, let alone figuring out a Profit and Loss Statement, or their own personal net worth for that matter. Such terms are foreign to them. Is it any wonder that college student loan obligations have now surpassed $1 trillion! Such loans must be paid back because they are immune from bankruptcy laws, except in some very special hardship cases. Student loans can even be attached to a Social Security check when the student retires, if they have not been expunged during their working life! Much of this could have been avoided with a proper understanding of how money works in our economy.

It is a sad commentary, that from an early age our young are taught by the indolent money masters how to sink into debt and pay high interest rates, in order to have what they want now, rather than saving for it. Once this psychological barrier is crossed, it is difficult to turn back, and borrowing against future earnings becomes a way of life. The problem is often further exacerbated by parents who pamper their kids. The idea of a kid working a part-time job to earn money is becoming quite unthinkable in many American families. Boy, how we have changed from the time I was a kid delivering newspapers at the age of ten!

How did we get into this mess? Is it indolence? Stupidity? Ignorance? Well, space does not allow me to go into great detail, but suffice it to say that when we went off the gold standard in 1971, our money was no longer backed by gold. This was the day in history when no circulating paper anywhere was redeemable in gold. Since then our government has been able to print money without any corresponding increase in our gross domestic product to justify it. We were given the status of the U.S. dollar becoming the world's reserve currency at the Bretton Woods Agreement in 1945, as a result of the ending of the Second World War that had devastated the economies of Japan, Germany, Great Britain, and most other European countries.

Today, many countries transfer their currencies into dollars in order to purchase oil and other commodities on the world market. This license to print money anytime we feel like it has led to dire consequences not only for America, but for the whole world. Since 2001 through 2008, America has spent well over one trillion dollars on wars alone, according to The National Priorities Project. A lot of our other debt has come from funding a high percentage of N.A.T.O., which is designed to protect Europeans. We also secure the homeland of Japan and other South East Asian nations. Our military armaments budget far outpaces the other nine countries in the top 10 armament producers. We also fund 23% of the United Nation's budget, and we are only one of 193 member nations. We have also become the de-facto "super cop" of the world, whereby we commit our military and our treasures to secure world order, while the B.R.I.C. nations of Brazil, Russia, India and China, appear to do very little other than protect their own interests. As a result, we have neglected our infrastructure, bridges, airports, and our highways are long overdue for upgrading. Meanwhile, a visit to many other major countries we helped after World War II, show strong vibrancy due to modern buildings, factories, and highways. It is a form of role-reversal I find very interesting.

So, with the funding of wars all over the world, and increasing our vast welfare system, we are here today facing a pile of debt. The final element concerns the fact that Americans have forgotten, or have never been exposed to, basic biblical principles regarding the smart way to manage money. If applied by our government, individuals and families, we may very well have avoided the dilemma we now face.

With respect to our government debt, the good news is that if we can grow our economy at 3% per annum or better, we can gradually reduce our sovereign debt exposure to a more acceptable number. Also, due to inflation reducing the value of our outstanding dollar debt every year, the debt ends up being devalued, and therefore easier to pay-off in the future. We can only pray that our leaders in Congress will eventually wrap their arms around this debt monster, and bring it under control once and for all.

The connective tissue that holds together the world's financial system over the centuries is not that hard to figure out. In the days of the Roman Empire, the two parties in a business transaction were often the master, (the Patricians), and the lower class, the (Plebeians). There were also a large percentage of slaves in both Rome and Athens. Later, in medieval times, the names of the parties changed to serf (farm laborer) and Lord (of the manor). Then, as a result of the British Industrial Revolution in the 18th century, the titles of the parties changed again to industrialist and laborer. In more enlightened times the parties became the employer and the employee. In each case, a job was created for the weaker of the two parties. The acronym JOB stands for Just Over Broke! It is a system whereby the employer pays the employee just enough to keep the employee viable, but never quite enough that would allow the employee to break from the system (unless he or she has become an astute money manager!). This system has allowed the dominant party to earn a profit from the production of the other party. Throughout all these times in history there has always been the creditor (lender), and the debtor (borrower), but in the pages of this book I am going to teach you how to reverse this relationship so you become the lender and not the borrower! I believe J. Paul Getty said it best, when he commented: "I'd rather have 1% of the effort of one hundred men, than 100% of my own effort!"

Today, creditors have fine-tuned their skills in such a sophisticated way, that Americans have been brain-washed into believing that debt is normal, and paying high rent (interest) for the privilege of borrowing, is as natural as breathing. One of the purposes of this book is to help you think of money in a totally different way, that will give you confidence in your own abilities to properly manage money by controlling it, saving it, and spending it according to Bible principles, i.e. God's principles.

The good news is that the financial crash of 2008 is now well behind us, and Americans and the economy in general have made significant gains since that time. Are we on the verge of a new golden age? Good economic progress continues to be made, and our job market is improving.

Qualifying for home mortgages is still a bit of a challenge for some, but progress is being made in this market as well. So, even though we still have some significant challenges ahead, you will find that now, more than ever, it is very important to wrap your mind around a good, thorough understanding of designing a plan to get out of debt and work towards a secure retirement.

Before I provide you with practical everyday solutions to your money management challenges, it is first important to develop your foundational thinking regarding money, the subject of Chapter One. Next, we take a careful look at the wrong way to manage money, and the traps to avoid in bringing money under the control of God's principles, the subject of Chapter Two. The power of giving is discussed in Chapter Three, and the role it plays in helping other less fortunate souls, while at the same time bringing us closer to God. Then, in Chapter Four, money basics are discussed, leading up to the personal budget process mentioned in Chapter Five. With the family budget firmly in place, the power of the double down debt reduction method, designed to tame the debt monster, is now reviewed in Chapter Six. How the credit system works, and the tools you can use to make it work for you, are the subject of Chapter Seven. Then, in Chapters Eight, Nine and Ten, I introduce you to assessing the tremendous profits and tax advantages of owning a small business, with the goal of accelerating your wealth holdings. You will soon realize that business ownership is one of the last great opportunities in America for the ordinary man or woman to enjoy true financial freedom. In Chapters Eleven and Twelve, I demonstrate a proven step-by-step plan that will save you thousands of dollars when you purchase big ticket items such as automobiles and real estate. Finally, in Chapters Thirteen, Fourteen and Fifteen, you are now ready and equipped to look at different types of investments that will guide you towards a financially free retirement, including how to make them grow, and how to protect them for the long term. By faithfully applying the strategies in this book, you can have the confidence of accumulating large savings, both in the near and long term, and that your money worries will finally be permanently brought under control.

SECTION ONE

THE SPIRITUAL SIDE OF MONEY

(The answer to an empty life is an empty tomb!)

CHAPTER ONE

BUILDING OUR FOUNDATIONAL THINKING

We are crucified between two crosses;
regret for yesterday, and fear of tomorrow!

– unknown

MARTIN LUTHER, the great theologian of the 16th century, once said that there are three conversions that take place in the Christian life. First there is a conversion of the heart, then the mind, and finally the purse (check-book). The point he was making is that the way we think about money and possessions are at the very heart of a good Christian life. So, the very best place to start is carefully studying God's word in the Bible itself.

BIBLE MONEY ROOTS

The whole premise of this book is based on proven, ageless money management principles that are found in one of the oldest books on earth, the Bible, which in our free society is readily available to anyone who wishes to read it, but unfortunately many people don't. That is not the case in many parts of the world, where a Bible is very hard to come by, and people have been known to expose themselves to great danger just to possess one. Upon reading it, you will find a treasure trove of good, sound advice about money management that has been forgotten in this modern age, and I want to bring to your attention these timeless principles which, when properly applied consistently in your life, will make an enormous difference in how you perceive and manage money. It will also provide you with peace of mind, and future prosperity that you may only have dreamed of. We are talking here about a transformation of your mind. With the right "head-set" on you can accomplish great financial success when you are working inside the principles of money management laid down by God Himself.

We all know that life without music would be much duller. Life without love would be very sad indeed. But a life without spiritual faith is stripped of any real meaning. Of the major world religions, only Christianity has maintained its full integrity despite the thorough investigation and analysis of Bible documents dating back thousands of years, and archeological digs that time and time again have confirmed the authenticity of Bible stories. Also, the Christian Bible is the only holy scripture, (of all major world religions), that has already confirmed more than 500 future prophecies, leading any rational person to believe that other prophetic events will come true in the future with the Second Coming of Jesus Christ. In my own studies, I have not discovered one prophetic event that has come true in the Islamic Qur'an, the India Holy Vedas, or the Buddhist Pali Canon (Tripitaka). Confirmed prophecies alone, makes the Bible the clear winner.

So, despite the fact that the Bible is the number one best-selling book in the world, why is it that many of its great wisdoms have been lost to modern man? We are going to explore, rekindle, and reacquaint you with what the Bible has to say about how we manage personal assets, and I believe that if you apply these principles consistently in your life, you will be well compensated as your just reward for being a faithful servant of God's assets. Yes, you did notice that I said "God's assets," and not yours. You are going to find many thoughts and comments in the Bible that may sound counterintuitive to you on the surface, until you dig deeper for their true meanings. Jesus' comments in the four gospels are good examples. As you pray and mediate on God's words to guide you, you will find hidden beauty of what He is trying to convey to you.

I realize that not everyone reading this book has read and studied the Bible, therefore a summary overview is perhaps warranted in order to set the stage for what I will be communicating to you later on. The Bible is actually a compendium of 66 books written by authors over a 1500 year time-span. These men were chosen and inspired by the Holy Spirit of God, to write down God's principles for the way man should live his life, for the short time he resides here on earth. As mentioned earlier, God uses the Bible effectively to say a great deal about money management.

The Bible is like a two-act play. There is the Old Hebrew Testament consisting of 39 books, followed by a silent period of some 400 years, which we will refer to as the intermission of the play. Then came the New Christian Testament consisting of 27 books that cover the time period of Jesus Christ's ministry here on earth, straight through to the modern age, and what we can expect in the future. The Old Testament is the New Testament concealed, and the New Testament is the Old Testament revealed. Both testaments go together like a horse and carriage. You can't have one without the other.

Unfortunately, and one of the main reasons for writing this book, is the fact that many Christians in America today are not reading the Bible regularly, and therefore make major decisions, not just financial, but other major life changing ones, without seeking God's input. Surveys indicate that half have not been to a church service in three months, although when they were growing up some 58% attended church regularly. Today, regular attendance is down to 27%! Also, only 40% believe in five or fewer of the Ten Commandments. Christianity today is alive and well, but unfortunately fewer people are listening to what God has to say than ever before in the history of our country. Therefore, I implore all readers, if they are not already doing so, to discipline themselves by listening to God. This means opening up the Bible regularly so that God can speak to your heart. The whole premise of this book is dependent on you embracing

God as your financial partner in making all future money decisions, by going first to prayer, and then to the Bible.

FOUNDATIONAL TENETS:

Before we delve too deeply into money management strategies, it is very important for us to establish a firm relationship with God with reference to how He wants us to manage money.

Therefore, we need to know certain foundational principles that we need to adhere to.

GOD WANTS YOU TO PROSPER!

Some people equate Christianity with poverty, but this is wrong. When you study the Bible you find that God wants you to be happy and to prosper. God does not expect His people to be poverty-stricken, living in rags, and worrying about their family's security. Remember that Jesus said: "I am come that they might have life, and that they will have it to the full." (John 10:10). Surveys of successful men have yielded the fact that they worked hard to reach their goals. From the very beginning, God has expected man to work diligently and reap the benefits of his hard work. The Fourth Commandment states that man should labor six-days and do all the work, but on the seventh day to rest. It is saying not only should we rest on the seventh day, but to "do all the work" during the other six days. God works and sustains our world, and he expects man to work hard also. God also tells us how to work: "Whatever your hand finds to do, do it with all your might." (Ecclesiastes 9:10). King Solomon said that the lazy man should study the ant, and how it works hard to save up food for the winter, even though there is no boss forcing him to do so (Proverbs 6:6-8). Also, St. Paul said that professing Christians who will not work are worse than unbelievers (I Timothy 5:8). Good hard work is evidence of being a good Christian!

Finally, on the subject of work, it is important to develop skills that make you valuable. Proverbs 22:29 states: "Do you see a man skilled in his work? He will serve before kings; he will not serve before obscure men." The word "skilled" also means "valuable," so you need to prepare for the best job you can. Therefore, be creative and explore all your options. Work for a firm that will not only pay you, but train you, or take night classes to master a trade etc. St. Paul also gave us instructions in making ourselves more valuable employees. He said we should be cooperative and zealous on the job, conscientiously serving our employer (Colossians 3:22-23; Titus 2:9). By working hard and becoming more valuable, you are in fact doing everything possible to not only keep your current job, but also to take advantage of future job promotions, or other opportunities that may come your way. Remember, you are working for God not man!

GOD OWNS IT ALL!

Have you ever coveted an asset, or boasted with pride that you owned it? This is the way the majority of the world's people think, so don't feel alone. The truth is, however, that God is the Creator of the whole universe and everything in it. Not only did He create everything, but He also owns everything as evidenced in Psalm 24:1, "The earth is the Lord's, and everything in it, the world and all who live in it; for He founded it upon the seas and established it upon the waters." God gets specific in Leviticus 25:23 when He declares that He owns all the land, and Haggai 2:8 defines asset ownership further when God stated: "The gold is mine and the silver is mine." Further, God also acknowledges in Psalm 50:10, "For every animal of the forest is mine, the cattle on a thousand hills." I could mention many more Bible verses on this subject, but the important point being made is that once we mentally and emotionally accept the universal fact that God owns everything, then we will begin to make every spending decision a spiritual decision. For instance, if you think that you own even a single asset, then that feeling of ownership will be reflected in your attitude. So, if something good happens to the asset then you will be pleased, but if something bad happens to the asset you will be upset. On the other hand, if you know the asset belongs to God who is in control of all things, then you will think much differently.

A good example of a man's Godly attitude towards possessions is to quote the great British preacher, John Wesley (1703 – 1791), who, upon learning that his house had just burned to the ground, commented: "The Lord's house burned; one less responsibility for me!" Wesley was not only acknowledging that the house belonged to God and not him, but he also had accepted the fact that God is in control of everything! One of his famous quotes was, "Gain all you can, save all you can, give all you can!" This is an English preacher that gave 42,000 sermons, an average of three a day. He traveled an average of 4500 miles each year, and at one point in his life, he was a missionary to American Indians. This is a man worth listening too!

Wesley was aware that God had promised to provide for his needs: "But seek first his kingdom, and his righteousness, and all these things will be given to you as well. Therefore, do not worry about tomorrow, for tomorrow will worry about itself. Each day has enough trouble of its own." (Matthew 6:33-34). You will also find in Philippians 4:19, where it says, "And my God will meet all your needs, according to his glorious riches in Christ Jesus." This Bible quote is saying that no matter how difficult a financial situation you find yourself in, you can be confident that God has promised to feed, clothe, and shelter you.

It is worth noting that most of the assets that we temporarily control actually belonged to someone else before we possessed them, and at some point in the future they will belong to someone else, especially after we leave this earthly existence. We actually control personal possessions for only a short period of time. The Bible has it right when it says: "Man born of woman is of few days and full of trouble. He springs up like a flower and withers away. Like a fleeting shadow he does not endure." (Job 14:1). So when it comes to money management, the very first Bible principle we need to understand and accept is that God owns everything!

WHAT ARE OUR RESPONSIBILITIES?

Now that we know what part God plays in our lives, we need to understand what our responsibilities are. God entrusts each and everyone one of us to be good stewards in the way we manage the assets He provides us. A good steward is a good manager of assets, and the role comes with great responsibilities. God is trusting us with temporary control over His assets, and we will be judged by how we manage them. The Bible states that faithfulness with our use of money will be rewarded, for it states: "His master replied, 'Well done, good and faithful servant! You have been faithful with a few things; I will put you in charge of many things. Come and share your master's happiness." (Matthew 25:23).

God tests us more than 200 times in the Bible, to determine our faithfulness to Him. In Luke 16:10-12, it says: "Whoever can be trusted with very little can also be trusted with much, and whoever is dishonest with very little will also be dishonest with much. So if you have not been trustworthy in handling worldly wealth, who will trust you with true riches? And if you have not been trustworthy with someone else's property, who will give you property of your own?" The great missionary, H.L. Hastings said it quite well when he stated: "Small things are small things, but faithfulness in small things is a big thing!"

The principle that God applies is simple. If we are faithful in a few things, God will put us in charge of many things. It is all a matter of turning everything over to God, and letting Him do his wonderful work in our life. We need to start maximizing God, and minimizing ourselves. We must make God greater in our lives, and ourselves smaller. God is the potter, and we are the clay. Let's put our ego to one side, and humble ourselves before God. After all, God will be holding us all accountable for our deeds once we die. (Romans 14:12). Why not try to live your life here on earth, for the short time you are here, the very same way you will when you get to heaven? Remember, foresight is better than hindsight, but insight is even better!

PRINCIPLES OF BEING A GOOD STEWARD

It should be pointed out that a good steward is faithful to his master in all things, including time, gifts, money, relationships, and employment. It isn't just about the money. It's a holistic attitude to everything we do. Stewardship, in other words, is the Christian life. In the parable of the talents, we find that God entrusts us all with different gifts, opportunities and financial assets. How we spend God's gifts to enhance His kingdom here on earth is where our accountability lies. If we waste our time, talents, and assets, rather than seek guidance from God in how we should proceed each day, then we face a reckoning later on.

In reading for yourself Jesus' parable of the talents (Matthew 25:14-30), and the parable of the ten minas (Luke 19:11-27), you will be immediately struck by the fact that God is the master and we are the servants. The master is the owner, and He has the final authority. The master has assigned trust and authority to the servant to be faithful in the way he manages the master's assets. The master has specific expectations of his servant, and the master makes it clear that the servant will be held accountable for his service to the master. Our role as servants, therefore, is very clear. We must place God's kingdom first by being responsible and faithful servants.

Try to imagine for a moment a heavenly bank account. When we do good deeds that are pleasing to God, we make a deposit, and when we sin there is a subtraction. In Matthew 6:19 we find Jesus saying: "Do not store up for yourselves treasures on earth, where moth and rust destroy, and where thieves break in and steal. But store up for yourselves treasures in heaven, where moth and rust do not destroy, and where thieves do not break in and steal. For where your treasure is there your heart will be also." We may not be able to take our assets with us when we die, but Jesus has clearly given us a way to send them on to heaven in advance of getting there!

Once we begin to implement a spiritual approach to money management, we gain contentment, as St. Paul alludes to in Philippians 4:19. Our aching, restless heart is replaced with a peace that surpasses all understanding. And as we begin to apply

God's rules of economy we will begin to see reductions in our debts, and we will be more prudent in how we spend. We will start a savings plan for our future security, and end up giving more than we ever have to the work of God. Now, if you are beginning to think of yourself as a money manager for God, you need to begin addressing what spiritual and financial changes you need to make in your life in order to prepare yourself for a future meeting with the Master. Remember also, that every Christian looks forward to being with Jesus, but when it does happen we will be stripped of all our worldly wealth whether we like it or not! The words of Jim Elliot, the missionary who was killed by natives in South America, ring loud and clear in my mind when he said: "He is no fool that gives what he cannot keep, to gain what he cannot lose." Putting it another way, an unknown writer once said, "Unless there is within us, that which is above us, we will soon yield to that which is around us!" So the second of God's principles is to be good and faithful stewards of God's assets.

PRAYER COMMENTS

I realize that not every reader is a Christian. I spent the first 30 years of my life living in darkness, before I found the light of Christ. Therefore, I am providing some input on the proper way to approach God in prayer if you are not already doing so. It involves five-steps:

1. It is important when we bow down to pray to God that we ask in faith. In the Book of James (1:6), it quotes: "But when he asks, he must believe and not doubt, because he who doubts is like the wave of the sea, blown and tossed by the wind."

2. When we pray we are to do it in Jesus' name. The Book of John (16:24), states, "Until now you have asked nothing in My name. Ask, and you will receive, and your joy will be complete."

3. It is also essential to understand that when we pray we are to do so according to God's will. I John (5:14), makes this point when it says, "This is the confidence we have in approaching God: that if we ask anything according to his will, he hears us."

4. We should not pray unless we are in a right relationship with others. This point is exemplified in I Peter (3:7), which says, "Husbands, in the same way be considerate as you live with your wives, and treat them with respect as the weaker partner and as heirs with you of the precious gift of life, so that nothing will hinder your prayers."

5. This last step is very important, in that when we pray we are not to have any unconfessed sin in our lives, as mentioned in Psalm (66:18), "If I had cherished sin in my heart, the Lord would not have listened."

CHAPTER TWO

WRONG THINKING TRAPS

Real wealth consists not in having many
possessions, but in having few wants
– Epicurus

I MENTIONED EARLIER that spiritual thinking about money is somewhat countercultural to American society's way of thinking. As such, further explanation is needed in order to counteract typical worldly views that must be overcome in order to partner with God for an eternal life beyond the one we are now living.

When we discuss spiritual ways of managing money and possessions, we find ourselves on opposite sides of the deeply entrenched thinking that has taken place in our worldly, capitalistic society. We need to change this way of thinking and start placing God's word above the false thinking of many in our population. To put matters into perspective, our $18 trillion dollar economy is the largest in the world, but 70% of it represents consumer goods to serve our 320 million population. This fact is startling when you consider that Americans comprise about five-percent of the world's population, yet we consume 20% of the world's goods and services, including 25% of all fossil fuel consumption. Meanwhile, according to the United Nations (UN.Org), 2.8 billion people survive on less than $2 per day, and 1.2 billion people live on $1 per day! Furthermore, almost

900 million people do not have enough to eat (that figure represents the populations of the United States, Europe and Canada combined!). Meanwhile, Americans eat plenty, with about 10% of their average monthly earnings being spent on food items. Compare this to a very food insecure country like Egypt, where the average family spends about 50% or more of their monthly income for food. Yes, Americans are very fortunate compared to most peoples in this world, and there is no denying that we are collectively a very generous people. Unfortunately, our generosity is not proportional, with some giving plenty, and others giving nothing at all. Many of our citizens place their own needs first out of ignorance of God's ways. We need to change this thinking and place God's words above the false thinking of many in our population.

THE ROOT OF ALL EVIL?

Many believe that money is the root of all evil, which is not true. Actually, it is the love of money that is the root of the evil, because when we love money it becomes an idol, and an idol is a substitute for God. I Timothy 6:10 confirms this point. We also find in Timothy 4:4-5 that: "For everything God created is good, and nothing is to be rejected if it is received with thanksgiving, because it is consecrated by the word of God and prayer."

We can use money for all kinds of things. We can use it to bribe someone, pay for illegal drugs, or use it to hurt others. In each case it is the person who is committing the evil, not the money.

Conversely, money can be used for good purposes like feeding the hungry, helping a distressed widow, or a friend who is destitute. Here again it is the person who is doing the good, not the money. Money is morally neutral. When we use money for honorable purposes, we know that God is very pleased as we are helping to build His kingdom.

In Luke 16:13 we find Jesus saying: "You cannot serve two masters ... You cannot serve both God and money." Therefore, we should not be serving money as it makes a poor master. However, when we use money for good purposes then we are making it a servant for good.

LOVING MONEY CAN BE DESTRUCTIVE

Our world is full of people who will do anything for money, and I mean anything! The grip that money can have on someone's life is not un-similar to an alcoholic or a drug addict that uses exploitive and devious means to get what they want. In James 4:2-3, it states: "You want something but you don't get it. You kill and covet, but you cannot have what you want. You quarrel and fight. You do not have, because you do not ask God. When you ask, you do not receive, because you ask with wrong motives, that you may spend what you get on your pleasures." How easy it is to fall into destruction, as we find in 1 Timothy 6:9, "People who want to get rich fall into temptation and a trap, and into many foolish and harmful desires that plunge men into ruin and destruction."

THE BATTLE BETWEEN MATERIALISM AND SPIRITUALISM

This battle is being fought every day, and far too often materialism wins out. It seems that the more money we possess, the more we want. Money is seductive and can lead to power and all types of other sins. However, when we realize that money will not buy us the contented soul that we seek, then God is given some fertile ground to bring us into His world. Materialism centers around obtaining money and possessions, rather than being God centered. Only God's ways can bring fulfillment as mentioned by Paul in his letter to the Philippians, mentioned earlier.

THE CURSE OF WEALTH

It is a biblical fact that it is very hard for a rich person to get into heaven. Jesus referred to money as a master that rivals the real master. This was exemplified in Jesus' story of the rich young man who did not follow Jesus because it meant giving up his wealth. Jesus goes on to say, "I tell you the truth, it is hard for a rich man to enter the kingdom of heaven. Again I tell you, it is easier for a camel to go through the eye of a needle than for a rich man to enter the kingdom of God." (Matthew 19:16-24). It is one of life's perplexing questions in trying to answer why humble, poor people who later acquire wealth, often turn from God. Such is the seductive influence of wealth. It's as though they have all their needs taken care of, and therefore don't need God anymore. Ezekiel 28:5 states it very clearly: "By your great skill in trading you have increased your wealth, and because of your wealth you heart has grown proud." There is nothing wrong being wealthy, provided we use our wealth wisely, and according to God's law. Then we are satisfying the spiritual aspects of asset ownership, and God will be pleased.

We should also keep in mind that the definition of being rich is not what it used to be. According to the Global Rich List, if you earn an annual income of more than $850.00 a year, you are richer than 50% of all the people in the world! Also, if you make more than $25,000.00 annually, you are in the top 10% of all the wage earners in the world! Rich is therefore a relative term.

In my travels into foreign countries, I have been told by very poor Christian people that we in America are the ones with the problems and challenges, due to the seductive nature of the affluence we enjoy, which puts distance between us and God. These poor people, on the other hand, have very little, often not knowing where there next meal is coming from. Therefore they are tested daily, and they live with God hour by hour trusting that He will provide. Therefore, they feel closer to God, and feel in their hearts that they are the blessed. Wow! This is much different than what the typical American would expect, but there is validity in what they say. We all tend to be somewhat ethnocentric in the way we think, but this story gives us pause to think deeper about such matters.

The Book of Revelation 3:17-21 sums up the curse of wealth very nicely when it says: "You say, 'I am rich; I have acquired wealth and do not need a thing.' But you do not realize that you are wretched, pitiful, poor, blind and naked. I counsel you to buy from me gold refined in the fire, so you can become rich . . . Those whom I love I rebuke and discipline. So be earnest, and repent. Here I am! I stand at the door and knock. If anyone hears my voice and opens the door, I will come in and eat with him, and he with me. To him who overcomes, I will give the right to sit with me on my throne..."

A MATERIALISTIC ATTITUDE CREATES GREED AND SELFISHNESS

The insecurity of people causes them to accumulate wealth out of fear, causing the evils of greed and selfishness to win the day. Enough is never enough, and instead of becoming more secure, their anxiety only heightens. Rather than storing up wealth here on earth they should be storing up treasures in heaven where it will be waiting for them when they later arrive. In the book of Ecclesiastes, we find a king who was given great wealth from God, but later withdrew from Him. This king tried all pleasures known to man, but in the end he declared: "Yet when I surveyed all that my hands had done, and what I had toiled to achieve, everything was meaningless, a chasing after the wind; nothing was gained under the sun."(Ecclesiastes . 2:11). At the end of the day, if a man has enjoyed three square meals, and is able to peaceably retire to his own bed with a roof over it, why should he not be content?

The Book of Proverbs contains many wonderful sayings about how we should live, and here is one I particularly like: "Keep falsehood and lies far from me; give me neither poverty nor riches, but give me only my daily bread. Otherwise, I may have too much and disown you and say, 'Who is the Lord?' Or

I may become poor and steal, and so dishonor the name of my God." (Proverbs 30:8-9).

MATERIALISM CREATES IMMORALITY

The quest for material gain lies at the heart of most illegal activity, but the majority of material gain is generally quite legal. Here again, it's all about how we view money. If we gain money legally with the understanding that it all belongs to God, and we understand our stewardship responsibilities, then there is nothing immoral to be concerned about. However, if we pursue material gain through illegal means in order to satisfy our selfish desires, or help negate our insecurities, then perhaps our attitude about money needs to be corrected.

A MATERIALISTIC VIEWPOINT RETARDS SPIRITUAL GROWTH

A man's pursuit of material gain can end up blinding him to his own spiritual poverty. What man is doing is making a fruitless attempt to find meaning in the gaining of wealth, rather than in the creator of all things, God. We have to remember that money cannot buy our salvation, and it will become useless when we face God. The Bible tells us very clearly, "Command those who are rich in this present world not to be arrogant nor to put their hope in wealth, which is so uncertain, but to put their hope in God, who richly provides us with everything for our enjoyment." (1 Timothy 6:17).

In summary, our normal belief system regarding the managing of money is diametrically opposite to God's, and until we reach a point of understanding that if God is not Lord over our wealth, then He is not our Lord. If you find yourself still struggling with some of the money concepts we have discussed so far, you may wish to ask God for wisdom in helping you to gain greater understanding. "If any of you lacks wisdom, he should ask God, who gives generously to all without finding fault, and it will be given to him." (James 1-5). Lastly, you have probably heard the phrase that it is better to give than to receive, but perhaps you have never had this concept thoroughly explained to you. Therefore, the next chapter is devoted to the importance of giving, and the many blessings you will receive when you obey God.

CHAPTER THREE

WHY GIVING IS SO IMPORTANT

It is far better to have enough for your need,
than to have enough for your greed!
– Gandhi

WE ALL ENJOY receiving gifts, but the Bible tells us that it is more blessed to give than to receive (Acts 20:35). We find in the Old Testament a great deal of attention being placed on the subject of giving. Interestingly, there are more verses about giving than any other subject on money matters. In fact, everywhere in the Bible you will find comments condemning covetousness and greed, whereas generosity and charity are promoted and encouraged.

DEVELOPING THE RIGHT ATTITUDE TOWARDS STEWARDSHIP

If we are to cultivate an attitude of giving, we must do so with love. Any other motivation other than love is wrong and does not benefit the giver. St. Paul stated it very well in I Corinthians 13:3 when he said: "If I give all that I possess to the poor and surrender my body to the flames, but have not love, I gain nothing." Part of the maturing process in becoming a total man or woman of God is to come to the realization that God has already blessed us in so many silent ways, that it is hard for us to comprehend. But as we grow older, we begin to gain insight into God's ways, which causes us to want to be more like Him. St. Paul went on to say: "When I was a child, I talked like a child, I thought like a child, I reasoned like a child. When I became a man, I put childish ways behind me." (I Corinthians 13:11).

A wonderful perspective to develop is to think of everything we give as a gift to God, rather than as a charitable donation. In this way, when we give it becomes more an act of worship rather than giving to the church or the poor as a form of charity. The reason we gift as a worship to God is to thank Him for everything that He has done and continues to do for us. As the creator of all things, He owns all things, and it is to His glory that we show our thanks through giving.

BENEFITS OF GIVING:

When we worship God with our giving, donations, tithing etc., He does not allow our gifts to go unnoticed in that we receive from God far more than we give. The gifts we receive from God are in His economy, and we may not necessarily benefit from the results in this life. However, we are building up credits in our heavenly bank account mentioned earlier.

Here are some examples:

Giving Frees us from the Power of Money

An interesting phenomenon happens when we give freely to the Lord. It helps us to lose our grip on money and the effects money has on our lives. This is worth repeating. Giving helps us to covet money less, and we gain the positive effects in everything we do. It becomes an antidote to greed and avariciousness, which can keep us from harm's way. "Be on your guard against all kinds of greed; a man's life does not consist in the abundance of his possessions." (Luke 12:15). We also find in Ecclesiastes 5:10: "Whoever loves money never has money enough; whoever loves wealth is never satisfied with his income. This too is meaningless." And Matthew 16:26 sums it all up very nicely: "What will it benefit a man if he gains the whole world yet forfeits his soul?"

Giving Develops our Character

As children of God we have been created in His image. Unfortunately, unlike Jesus who was unselfish, we are born by nature to be very self-centered. Therefore, in order to be more like God in our hearts and attitudes, we need to give consistently in order to change our attitudes from a selfish perspective to one of sincerely wanting to provide for our fellow man, who may have far less than we do. This life is very inequitable. Some people enjoy fortunes while others go begging for their next meal. There is no justice in this world, and there never will be. We must wait for heaven to see it. Meanwhile, we have an obligation to do God's work while we live on this planet, by allowing God to use us as His instruments to help others who are less fortunate. Giving is the most effective response to the human disease of covetousness. God even has a solution for the rich and those who have surplus to share when He states in I Timothy 6:17: "Command those who are rich in this present world not to be arrogant or put their hope in wealth, which is so uncertain, but to put their hope in God, who richly provides us with everything for our enjoyment. Command them to do good, to be rich in good deeds, and to be generous and willing to share. In this way they will lay up treasures in heaven for themselves as a firm foundation for the coming age, so that they may take hold of the life that is truly life." (emphasis mine).

Giving gets us Closer to God

When we give on a consistent basis, it helps us to think more about Jesus. This helps us to concentrate and direct our hearts on Jesus rather than ourselves, and this brings us closer to Him. Matthew 6:21 states it clearly, "For where your treasure is, there your heart will be also."

Giving Increases Material Blessings

There are several Bible verses stating when you give generously, the Lord will bless you materially providing you have the right attitude. Before I go further I must emphasize the importance of giving with the right heart, otherwise there is no gain for the giver. However, if a giver follows what the Bible says about giving, as mentioned previously, then the following verses definitely apply:

> "One man gives freely, yet gains even more; another withholds unduly, but comes to poverty." (Proverbs 11:24-25). We are reminded of this further in II Corinthians 9:6 "Remember this. Whoever sows sparingly will also reap sparingly, and whoever sows generously will also reap generously. Each man should give what he has decided in his heart to give, not reluctantly or under compulsion, for God loves a cheerful giver."

God and only God has the right to instruct us how to spend. With this point in mind, it may be a better attitude on our part to ask how much of God's money should I keep for myself, rather than asking, how much of my money should I give to God? Because man is naturally covetous, he has often robbed God and kept for himself. God discusses this very matter in Malachi 3:8-10, when he says: "Will a man rob God? Yet you rob me. But you ask, 'How do we rob you?' God replied: "In tithes and offerings. You are under a curse – the whole nation of you – because you are robbing me. Bring the whole tithe into the storehouse, that there may be food in my house. Test me in this," says the Lord

HOW MUCH SHOULD WE GIVE?

We find in the Old Testament that God mentioned a sum of ten-percent of our income as a tithe. This is mentioned in Malachi 3:8-9, and Leviticus 27:30, for instance. We also find that the ancient Hebrews gave other sacrificial offerings, as mentioned in Deuteronomy 12:17. The sum total of these offerings amounted to well over 20% of their income. Hebrews were also told to forgive debts owed to them every 50 years (Jubilee).

The New Testament is a little less clear in that it says we should give according to the material blessings we have received. This lack of specific clarity places emphasis on the relationship each of us has with God. Many mature Christians, after years of prayer have concluded that a tithe of ten-percent of our income is a good start, but they strive to give more wherever possible. Using ten-percent as a base makes it easy to figure, and allows us to be consistent with application of the tithe. We should also remember that tithing is personal. It is no one else's business other than our Lord. Therefore, when we give we should not discuss it with others, unless we are teaching a child or a new believer.

IS THERE A REASON FOR NOT GIVING?

It is easy to rationalize not tithing part of our income. Many people claim there is too much month left after the money is spent. Therefore, how can they possibly incur another debt on top of everything else they are burdened with? The truth is they really don't want to tithe, and here is proof. If you ask such a person what would they do if they incurred a ten-percent pay cut, they undoubtedly would agree that they would somehow get by. This proves that they can pay a tithe. In recent years, due to the economic crisis of 2008, many families have experienced job losses or in some cases cut backs in hours resulting in 30%, 40%, or even 50% cuts in family income, yet they have still managed to tithe and be faithful to the Lord. It is all a matter of priorities. If we have already accepted the fact that all we possess belongs to God, and He will always provide for us, then we are demonstrating a lack of trust in God when we don't tithe. Is it not better to be inside God's favor rather than going against His will? Later, in this book, I will be providing you ways to improve your personal financial position. However, in order for it to happen we must not only apply self-discipline to follow through on our commitments, but we must always remember who is really in charge, and that giving to the Lord first, in order to help those less fortunate than ourselves, is at the center of the matter. Remember also that giving less due to temporary circumstance, such as a job loss, should not at the same time diminish your faith to give what you can.

WHOM SHOULD WE GIVE TO?

Our giving should be shared in three circumstances:

Our Family

In the last 50 years or so we have been witness to a tragic breakdown in family values resulting in parents neglecting or not providing for their children, and adults who have failed to provide for their parents in old age. The Bible, however, condemns such practices: "If anyone does not provide for his relatives, and especially for his immediate family, he has denied the faith and is worse than an unbeliever." (I Timothy 5:8). The family is the basic structural unit that holds our society together, yet, instead of reinforcing it our society is tearing it apart. The family unit is continuously under attack and must be preserved at all costs. If it falls apart, everyone fails including society as a whole. Let us never forget that charity begins at home.

The Church and Other Christian Ministries

A very good case can be made that we should support our local church with our tithing as this is the place where we receive soul nourishment, and it keeps us accountable. Normally, provided our family is taken care of, our "first fruits" should be to help our church. I Timothy 5:17 states that our elders who are good leaders should be worthy of an ample honorarium, especially those who work hard at preaching and teaching. Supporting our local Christian church helps to provide a positive environment not only for the church body, but also for the local community where we live. Any other ministries we decide to support, such as missionaries, charities etc., should be over and above our church tithe.

Providing for the Poor

Some 2,000 years ago, Jesus said that the poor will always be with us. Despite President Lyndon Johnson's declared war on poverty back in 1965, American tax payers have spent more than $20 trillion in attempting to stamp out poverty in America. Today, however, we have about the same poor statistics we had in 1965. Jesus was clearly right. Does this mean we are not supposed to help the poor from our personal possessions? Absolutely not!

In fact, helping the poor is at the very heart of Christianity. In the B.C. era we find there was little help for the poor, but with the advent of the Christian movement it has become traditional for churches to help the unfortunate poor. Moreover, today there are also numerous non-profit Christian corporations that do an excellent job of assisting the poor with the donations they receive from the general public. Be sure, however, to thoroughly check them out before donating. I use the rule of thumb that no more than 20% of total revenues should be used to cover salaries, and overhead. The other 80% should go directly to fulfill the mission and purpose of the charitable organization. You may wish to first visit a charity watchdog such as: www.charitynavigators.org, who annually review the financial statements of numerous charity organizations, and then provide a rating. This provides transparency so you know how your hard earned money is being used. This approach provides integrity to the system.

With the growth of the federal government, and the introduction of numerous welfare programs to help poor families, we find today that the definition of being poor in America is not the same as being poor in many of the developing nations of the world. The global death rate of children under the age of five was well over six million in 2013, which represents about 17,000 per day according to www.womenandchildrenfirst.org.uk, About one-third of those deaths are a direct result of malnutrition. I mentioned earlier that more than 900 million people around the world do not have enough to eat, yet the USDA released in February 2014, a 2010 report that showed some 31% or 133 billion pounds of the 430 billion pounds of food available went uneaten! I mention these statistics to show the need to give to the poor globally as well as domestically.

There are specific admonitions in the Bible that clearly cry out for us all to be helping the poor. The following Bible verses should be read slowly and carefully in order to allow God's word to dig deep into our souls: "He who is kind to the poor lends to the Lord, and He will reward him for what he has done." (Proverbs 19:17). You will also find a longer passage in Matthew 25:34-45, where God clearly states His views to mankind with reference to helping people who are in distress - the poor, the hungry, the thirsty, the naked, the stranger, the prisoner. I believe this passage will do you more good if you read it for yourself as there is a definite price to pay for disobeying this Godly admonition.

It might also be the case that if we ignore the needs of the poor, it may very well entail not receiving answers to our prayers. It says in Isaiah 58:7-9, "Is it not to share your food with the hungry, and to provide the poor wanderer with shelter – when you see the naked to clothe him, and not to turn away from your own flesh and blood? Then your light will break forth like the dawn, and your healing will quickly appear; then your righteous-ness will go before you, and the glory of the Lord will be your rear guard. Then you will call, and the Lord will answer."

SECTION TWO

THE MANAGEMENT
OF MONEY

*(True happiness flows from the possession of wisdom and
virtue, and not from the possession of external goods!)*
– Aristotle

CHAPTER FOUR

MONEY BASICS

What is the safest way to double your money?
Fold it over and keep it in your pocket!
– Groucho Marx

IN OUR CAPITALISTIC society we find that everything we touch is either money, or one step removed from money. The days of farming for our own food, and surviving using our own ingenuity are gone. Today, money is used in exchange for all our worldly needs. It is a commodity, but it is not wealth. Just because someone claims to have money does not mean anything in and of itself. That same person may have debts that exceed the value of their money and other assets. There is no question, however, that our lives can be made much easier with adequate amounts of money and no debts. This point gets to the heart of personal money management. It's all about managing our money in a Godly fashion in order to achieve specific goals, both here and in eternity, while at the same time avoiding the many pitfalls associated with acquiring wealth.

MONEY PERFORMS FOUR FUNCTIONS:

1. It serves as a medium of exchange, meaning that people are willing to swap it for other goods, which makes it far more efficient that bartering.

2. Money represents a unit of accounting, which allows businesses to place a specific price on economic goods and services.

3. It functions as a store of value or purchasing power.

4. It also acts as a standard of deferred payment, thus allowing for long periods of time to pay-back, and to conduct business over great geographical distances.

In order to perform all of the above functions, money always has to be available, durable, affordable, fungible, portable, and most importantly, reliable. In the past, the main forms of commodity money were gold and silver, but today people are willing to accept paper currency, coins, and balances in transaction accounts (i.e. bank checking accounts etc.,).This is called fiat money, which means it is simply paper money that is not backed by gold, but rather the full faith and pledge of the United States Treasury to honor it.

One wonders why people today are willing to accept a commodity that has no intrinsic value. After all, it is not easy to sell checks for use as raw materials in the manufacturing process. The reason is that payments arise from a fiduciary monetary system, which means that the general public has confidence that such payments can be exchanged for goods and services. Therefore, dollar value is based on public confidence, but there is nothing to back it up as collateral.

Money is also a liquid asset, meaning that it can be readily converted in exchange for other things. Some assets, however, are not easily converted into cash. Real Estate is a good example of a non-liquid asset that must either be sold or refinanced in order to put your hands on the money tied up in the real estate's bricks and concrete. A dollar bill, on the other hand, is easily convertible into other things. For instance, it is estimated that a dollar bill transfers more than 50 times per year from one consumer to the next, the most liquid commodity of all.

FOUR THINGS YOU NEED TO KNOW ABOUT MONEY:

There are many characteristics of money, but we should know the following four as they are foundational to all investment decisions we make.

How Money Depreciates in Value

The famous economist, Milton Friedman, once said that inflation is taxation without representation! Why? Because money depreciates without us doing anything about it. Since the Federal Reserve Banking System was enacted back in 1913, we have witnessed a devaluation of the dollar making it worth about five-percent of its original value. This happens because inflation increases the cost of living each year, and therefore it takes more of today's dollars to buy things in the future. That is why it is so important to invest our money at a rate of return that is higher than the inflation rate, which hovers around 3% per annum. Below is an illustration of how inflation reduces our purchasing power:

Inflation Reduction in Purchasing Power over Ten Year

2 percent	-18%
4 percent	-32%
6 percent	-44%
8 percent	-54%
10 percent	-61%

Table 4:1

Use of a good inflation calculator can be of immense help in showing you not only the value of what $1,000.00, or any amount, will be 20 years from now using a 3% inflation factor, but also what the value of $1,000.00 will have to become 20 years from now in order to maintain the same value. In chapter fourteen I provide an example of how to plan your retirement figures taking into consideration inflation so that you end up with a realistic idea of what to aim for.

How Money Appreciates in Value

In order for money to appreciate in value it must be invested at an annual interest rate that exceeds the annual rate of inflation. Investing in appreciable assets, such as real estate, is a much better investment than purchasing a new, fancy car that will depreciate tremendously the moment you drive it off the lot.

The Rule of 72 – A Simple Method to Calculate Rates of Return

The Rule of 72 is a simple short-cut that makes it very easy to figure the time value of money. By dividing 72 by the rate of return on your chosen investment, you obtain the number of years it takes to double your money. For instance, if you expect to receive a 7.0% annual rate of return, then it will take 10.2 years for your investment to double in value.

How to Monitor Inflation

Inflation is the silent killer of money value. To understand it, you need to familiarize yourself with the CPI (Consumer Price Index), which is published every month by the Bureau of Labor Statistics, and is free for anyone to see. It provides data on changes in the prices paid by urban consumers for a representative basket of goods and services. The country is divided up by regions to allow for the cost of living differences in different states. This is how the government measures inflation in our economy. You can learn more by going to www.bls.gov. The figures you obtain are useful for negotiating an annual wage increase, and doing a better job of working your family budget, which is the next subject we will discuss.

Unfortunately, understanding the aforementioned money rules is not enough. We also have to understand ourselves, in how we justify the spending of money. So let's look at a number of other issues that play a critical role in how we grow our money.

MONEY MANAGEMENT PITFALLS

Let's start by pointing out some of the challenges we all face in managing money:

Not Planning

Deadlines are established to ensure things get done on time. With personal money management, however, there are no deadlines for retirement unless you make one, and that is a problem. You can allow credit card debt to accumulate, pay higher taxes unnecessarily, and of course keep putting off planning for retirement. At some point, however, you must decide to plan, because if you don't, then you have already arrived, because you will be in the same place five-years from now!

Overspending

There is a real tendency for all of us to spend money without realizing the true consequences of our actions. The result is overspending, which can lead to heavy debt that cannot be retired by the next couple of paychecks. This leads to interest charges, causing us to pay more for what we purchased than what we intended.

Emotional Decision Making

Succumbing to emotions when we make decisions about money can result in lots of heartache later on. Impulse buying is promoted heavily by retailers causing us to think that this deal cannot be passed up. It is so important to resist these impulses and use the power of reason every time we spend money, especially on costly items.

Delaying Crucial Decisions

Many people are so absorbed in the now moment that they often neglect or put-off crucial action points that need to be made each week and month throughout the year, if they ever expect to make progress in getting ahead.

Not Planning for the Unexpected

No one likes surprises, but if we fail to plan in advance, then Murphy's Law will always pay us a visit. It is important to create an overall awareness of not only your current financial obligations, but also those extracurricular one-time expenses that rear their ugly heads now and again in order to create chaos in the family budget.

Not Doing Your Homework

Don't be lazy when money decisions have to be made. Search for information, and shop around. Think about how much money you can save in one-year by adding this one extra step!

Family Misunderstandings

Parents are sometimes at odds with each other regarding spending and saving. This can lead to stressful relationships, which can cause them to go around in circles without making progress. Therefore, it is important that they recognize their own strengths as well as weaknesses, and agree to a formula that will work for both parties. If parents do not agree on a financial plan for the family, then they have no plan. And if they have no plan then a good quality retirement is put into jeopardy. Financial planning is a shared responsibility. It takes two to tango.

Exposing Yourself to Catastrophic Risk

You make your family vulnerable if you don't take the steps to protect them through insurance coverage. People without a substantial savings account, or a support system, may find themselves homeless through accidents or medical issues.

Money represents the "grease" that turns the "wheels" of our capitalistic economy. Therefore, the more we learn about the attributes of money: how to earn it, how to keep it, how to protect it, how to invest it, and most importantly, knowing the rules for being a good steward with the money God has entrusted us with, are life-long lessons that the earlier we start to learn them, the better!

CHAPTER FIVE

A PERSONAL BUDGET PROCESS THAT REALLY WORKS!

I'm living so far beyond my means,
you could say we are living apart

– E.E. Cummings

SO FAR ON our journey we have discussed the importance of getting the "right head-set" on when it comes to managing our money and other assets. Hopefully we now all agree that all of our assets actually belong to God and not to us. We are the temporary custodians of God's assets, and as long as we control them we have a stewardship responsibility to manage them to the best of our knowledge and capabilities in a partnership with God. We have learned the importance of prioritizing, by giving to church and charities first, to promote God here on earth while also helping our fellow man. This is an extremely important concept to not only understand, but to also implement in our everyday lives.

I can't emphasize enough the importance of pointing out that God is always testing us to determine our faithfulness. As I mentioned earlier, there are some 200 instances in the Bible where God tests us. Have you ever wondered why? Why does God bother to test us if there is no other life after this one? 200 tests is no small number, and it demonstrates how important this issue is to God. We need to make this matter equally as important to ourselves. There is no doubt that the test of giving lies somewhere towards the top of the list of testing priorities that God creates for us.

Before we discuss the budgeting process, I want to take just another moment to put some perspective on the way we handle money that comes into our possession. Our definition of poverty in America is much different than the definition across most of the world. In America if you live in a home with a good roof, a couple of cars in the drive-way, access to air-conditioning, potable drinking water, electricity, wide-screen TV, and a refrigerator loaded with food, you can be considered poor by our government's definition of poverty. This should give us pause to thank God for whatever we do have, and if we have to do a little budget "belt-tightening" and sacrificing in order to get our finances in order, so that we can look forward to a great retirement, then it is a small price to pay for the big pay-off later on.

THE PERSONAL FAMILY BUDGET

Many small businesses fail because they don't have a business plan, and do not budget properly. Individuals and families are no different. A family, when you think about it, is running a small business. There are revenues to be produced, expenses to be paid, and planning budgets both for the short and long term. Don't be like a ship without a rudder, wandering aimlessly across a sea of uncertainty, just waiting for the next big wave to sink you under. Take control. You will feel much better.

Here are a few sample goals to consider:

1. Start your own business.
2. Retire from renting and own your own home.
3. Pay-off all your credit cards and other bills to get out of debt.
4. Prepare yourself for taking care of your parents or an invalid child one day.
5. Travel the world and complete your "bucket list."

6. Help others less fortunate than yourself.

7. Ensure your family is OK if anything happens to you.

8. Obtain better control of your finances to eliminate worry.

9. Work towards a solid plan for a dignified retirement.

10. Complete your education or the education of a child.

Determining which goals fit your emotional make-up is an important first step. Then, by putting the numbers down on paper you will find it to be psychologically rewarding in that it puts a realistic face on the challenges that must be tackled to reach your goals.

Is it Necessary to Budget?

When we establish guidelines to determine where our money goes, we can in actual fact make our money stretch further. So, when you think about it, a personal budget is our own plan for the wise spending of the money God has blessed us with, by putting it to maximum effective use in achieving our goals.

My experience in helping others is that expenses always seem to rise a little higher than income. You might attribute this to the confidence factor that life will continue as usual, and we will fix the problem later. Unfortunately, many people don't face up to the problem until there is a crisis, or they have to sacrifice something because they can no longer afford to purchase it. Then they act. To be forewarned is to be forearmed. Planning ahead helps us avoid such trying experiences.

A Necessary First Budget Step

In order to create a realistic family budget, it is important to keep track of all your expenses for the next 30 days. This is a team effort. Both husband and wife need to track their spending on every item spent. If you are a student, then it helps to share your goals with your parents so they can keep you accountable – just for 30 days!

All you need is a small notebook where you place the day and the date at the top. Then, simply set-up a horizontal column, that shows what you purchased, how you purchased it (cash, debit, credit card or check), and the amount. At the far right you should also bracket the letters (N) and (W). This indicates whether the expenditure was a WANT or a NEED! This will help you later to determine your emotional approach to impulse spending. It is also important to develop the habit of praying before you spend on each item, at least during the 30 day period, but even better if you make it a life-long habit. This process acts as a double-check on your thinking, because you are checking in with headquarters (heaven) before you actually make the decision to spend the money. All adults should participate, and share their findings. Remember also that this is not an exercise to render judgment, but to assess the reality of how money is being spent. Adjustments can always be made later.

Date	Day	Amount	Purchase Explanation	How Paid	(N)	(W)	Totals
12/6	Wednesday	$ 5.65	Starbucks Coffee	Cash		(W)	$ 5.65
12/6	Wednesday	$36.98	Gasoline fill-up	Debit Card	(N)		$36.98
12/7	Thursday	$22.65	Dinner with friends	Mastercard		(W)	$22.65
12/8	Friday	$11.00	Babysitting cost	Cash		(W)	$11.00
12/9	Saturday	$56.50	Wife's Clothing	Check # 6	(N)?	(W)?	$56.50

Figure 5.1 Daily Worksheet of Expenditures

When it comes to budgeting it should also be pointed out that expenses fall into three types: 1) fixed expenses, which include things like rent or mortgage payments; charitable giving, insurance, utilities etc., 2) Variable expenses that can change from month to month i.e. clothing, minor car repairs, and food (some months have five-weeks for instance), and 3) extracurricular expenses, which are referred to as periodic expenses, such as: heavy car or home repairs, health emergencies, summer camp for the kids etc. So the challenge is to design a budget that captures all three of the above expense categories so that your budget is not damaged when periodic expenses occur.

Establishing Your Net Worth

While you are tracking your income and expenses during the 30 day period, you also need to create a Balance Sheet to determine what you own and what you owe. Assets are what you own, and liabilities are what you owe. By adding up your assets and then subtracting your liabilities you create either a surplus number, which we call equity or net worth. Or, if you end up with more liabilities than the value of your assets, then you have a negative net worth. This is a polite way of saying you are, at the moment, technically bankrupt until you turn matters around. This exercise provides a big picture overview of where you stand financially at a certain point in time. Here is a typical example:

Jack and Betty Rae Wilson
BALANCE SHEET as of: _____

ASSETS		LIABILITIES	
Personal Checking Account	$ 345.00	Home Mortgage	$ 175,500.00
Personal Savings Account	$ 7,345.00	Home Second Mortgage	$ 10,000.00
Stocks /Mutual Funds	$ 3,000.00	Jack's Car Loan	$ 8,000.00
Value of Home	$ 205,000.00	Betty Rae's Car Loan	$ 6,500.00
Value of Jack's Auto	$ 8,500.00	Master Card	$ 4,400.00
Value of Betty Rae's Auto	$ 6,900.00	Visa Card	$ 2,700.00
Cash Value of Life Insurance	$ 4,000.00	CITI Card	$ 2,100.00
Brother-in-Law Note Owed	$ 2,000.00	Boat Loan	$ 8,900.00
Value of Gold/Silver Coins	$ 6,000.00		
Value of Stamp Collection	$ 8,000.00		
Value of Boat	$ 7,000.00		
TOTAL ASSETS	$ 258,090.00	TOTAL LIABILITIES	$ 218,100.00

Figure 5.2 Personal Balance Sheet

In this example, the Wilsons have a positive net worth or equitable position of $39,990.00 ($258,090.00 minus $218,100.00), so you can make the case that they are in the clear. However, this is not quite true. Depending on the quantity and quality of income coming into the household, meaning not only the total amount, but also the confident predictability, or quality, of the future income stream, this family could be in trouble now or in the near future. In business we use the rule of thumb that there should be $2 in assets for every $1 in liabilities, which is clearly not the case here. This family has over-leveraged their assets, which makes them vulnerable in the event of some emergency or loss of job. Clearly the family has done a number of things right in accumulating over $250,000.00 in assets, but the equity in their home is very thin, and the credit card balances are not being paid off every month, thus subjecting them to unnecessary high interest costs. A case could therefore be made to possibly sell the boat, gold, silver, and stamp collection, and use the money to pay-off high interest credit card debt. This would be a good start. We will be discussing other ways to reduce debt and increase our assets in later chapters.

Creating Your Own Family Budget

Let us assume for the moment that you have kept track of your spending for the last 30 days. You have carefully assessed how much you have spent, what you spent the money on, and determined if each expenditure was a Want or a Need. You have also established your net worth position to determine if it is positive, with a surplus of asset value over your liabilities, or that your liabilities exceed the value of your assets creating a negative net worth.

The next important step in the process is to complete the personal budget worksheet in Figure 5.4. Before we do so, however, I want to familiarize you with the numbers in Figure 5.3 that will provide you with average American household budget costs, which you can use as a guideline for your own budget assessments.

AVERAGE U.S. HOUSEHOLD BUDGET GUIDELINES

The Consumer Income and Expenditure Survey, which is conducted each year by the U.S. Bureau of Labor Statistics, provides us with very good information that allows us to compare our own situation against the average U.S. household for both income and household expenses. This exercise acts as an anchor allowing us to compare our situation against the American average. It is similar to a business comparing its Profit & Loss Statement against its peer group's composite average in the same industry.

The CE survey refers to the average income and expenditures per consumer unit (the definition of a consumer unit includes families, single persons, living alone, or sharing a household with others, but who are financially independent, or two or more persons living together who share expenses). These figures are illustrated in Figure 5.3.

Average Income of all Consumer Units	2013	2014	2015	% Change 2013-2014	2014 - 2015
Average income before taxes	$63,784	$66,877	$69,629	4.8	4.1

These household income figures can be further isolated by region of the country in which you live. Remember also that the numbers are average, meaning half the households earn more and half earn less that the figures shown. Differences in income occur due to education levels, special occupational skills, and region of the country where you reside. Economic trends also sometimes favor some occupational incomes over others.

AVERAGE LINE ITEM EXPENDITURES EXPLAINED:

As mentioned earlier, the main reason for doing a monthly budget is because debts can easily exceed income earned, and we want to reverse this reality so we can begin the accomplishment of reaching our goals. Naturally, if you typically have monthly income surpluses, you can concentrate on your investment portfolio, and plan for the future.

Average Household Budget Expenses in the U.S. (2015)

As mentioned, the average pre-tax income in the U.S. by household, was $69,629.00 in 2015, and according to the Consumer Expenditure

Survey for the same year, you can readily see in Figure 5.3 how the average household budget breaks out. Some readers may carefully question some of the numbers. Realize, however, that these numbers are average, and vary among different regions of the country. You can obtain more localized numbers from the Bureau of Labor if you wish to dig deeper. Meanwhile, the purpose in showing you the above numbers is to provide you with some perspective when preparing your own budget by showing your strengths in any one spending category, and perhaps also your weak points.

Average Cost of Housing

The average of $18,409.00, mentioned below, includes all costs pursuant to housing, which includes an average of $10,742.00, for payment of rent, or mortgage, property taxes, and insurance. The remaining amount includes utilities: electric, heating and cooking fuels, water, sewer, septic, trash collection, phone service (including cell phones), and home security services. Average utility costs are about $320.00 per month. Also, some 71% of households spend $1,600.00 on average for services that may include eldercare, babysitting, house cleaning, lawn service, laundry cleaning, pest control, and dry cleaning. Approximately 64% of householders own their own home, with about 50% owing a mortgage. The remaining 35% of households that rent pay a little less than homeowners each year for their rent, maintenance costs, and renters insurance.

Figures include a wide range of rents that include smaller towns as well as large metropolitan centers. Based on the numbers it appears to be a myth that renters are throwing away their money, because homeowners actually spend more on non-returnable costs in every area of the country with the exception of the South. Buying a home only seems to pay-off if you own for at least three-years with a fixed rate mortgage, while rents continue to climb. Also, owning a home also provides the opportunity for appreciation of value.

Average Transportation Costs

This cost is usually the second largest expense item for most households at $9,503.00 for 2015.

About 90% of all households report spending money for gasoline at an average of $3,000.00 per year, or about $250.00 a month. Auto insurance averages about $907.00 per year. About 20% of households regularly pay for public transportation averaging about $225.00 per month. Other transportation costs include car payments, costs of vacations, and seasonal events when purchasing plane tickets, intercity buses, train, and ship fares.

Average Food Costs

U.S. households pay an average of 10% of their income for food costs. The remainder is for food we eat outside of the home. We are told the poorest of American households, those earning less than $15,000.00 per year, spend an average of $3,500.00 annually on food, and eat out far less. At the opposite end of the income figures, those households earning more than $70,000.00 per year, spend an average of 10,000.00 per year, and tend to eat out 45% of the time.

EXPENDITURE CATEGORY		AVERAGE ANNUAL COST
Average Income before taxes		$ 69,629.00
Average Annual Expenditures		$ 55,978.00
Food		$ 7,023.00
At home	$ 4,015.00	
Away from home	$ 3,008.00	
Housing		$ 18,409.00
Shelter	$ 10,742.00	
Utilities	$ 3,885.00	
Household furnishings	$ 1,818.00	
Apparel & Services		$ 1,846.00

Transportation		$	9,503.00
Vehicle Purchases	$ 3,997.00		
Gas & Motor Oil	$ 2,090.00		
Healthcare		$	4,342.00
Health Insurance	$ 2,977.00		
Entertainment		$	2,842.00
Education		$	1,315.00
Cash Contributions		$	1,819.00
Personal Insurance and Pensions		$	6,349.00
Life and other Personal Insurance	$ 333.00		
Pension and Social Security	$ 6,016.00		
All Other Expenditures		$	2,530.00

Figure 5.3 BLS tells us that these numbers do not add up to 100% and due to variables per households, some sub-numbers do not equal the total in the right hand columns

Average Social Security, Personal Insurance, and Pension Contributions

Typical households spent $6,016.00 in 2015 in order to protect its members from poverty in old age, or due to disability or death. The majority of the expense is for Social Security payments, which accounts for 77% of all households. Self-employed people pay both the employer and employee amounts directly to the government via self employment taxes. Smaller percentages of households also pay into government railroad or private retirement plans. More than one in four U.S. households either have life insurance, annuity, or other personal insurance, at an average cost in excess of $1,200.00 per year.

Average Taxes Paid

Average household taxes amounted to $8,094.00 for 2015, and this does not include property tax, gasoline, or sales tax. The largest amount goes to the federal government, which does not include Social Security or Medicare payments. On average, taxes are about 12% of household incomes.

Average Health Care Costs

Health care costs have risen considerably of late, but for 2015 the average household paid about $4,300.00 in annual costs. The federal government has claimed that health care insurance is affordable if premiums cost no more than 9.5% of a household's modified adjusted gross income. If it rises above that level, then individuals and families qualify for subsidies if they purchase insurance on the federal or state health insurance exchanges. As of this writing, a lot of changes are expected to happen in the near future, so it is important to keep abreast of those changes in order to purchase the best health care plan possible in your area of the country.

A SPECIAL NOTE ON HIGHER EDUCATION COSTS

Conspicuous by its absence from the above budget numbers is a category for college costs for your children. The reason this budget item was left out, is not only because it is discretionary (you can make a conscious decision not to fund), but also because a college education today is not what it used to be. In earlier times, a young man or woman would go to college to learn how to think for themselves, and learn about God. They were educated liberally in the classic meaning of the term, spanning the whole vista of human knowledge: mathematics, English literature, sciences, foreign languages, history, and so on. Colleges not only created the Renaissance person, they also placed great emphasis on teaching students about the spiritual side of their own nature. In this way, Christian principles for living were clearly inculcated into the young person's psyche, which helped them to later use good judgment concerning their life careers, who they should marry, and how to become a leader in the community. This way of thinking has been replaced by many university faculty members, who are now teaching in a more humanistic, secular environment. This approach puts greater distance between the student and God, and therefore more of a spiritual disconnect. Many parents do not want this to happen, especially after experiencing heavy savings depletion, or going into debt for the privilege.

Today, college students learn more and more about less and less, because specialization is the norm of the day. They may learn about computers, but they could not tell you who wrote the classic, *War and Peace,* or what the capital of China is. There is also a great disconnect between the degree majors being offered versus the job market availability. There are simply too many "soft" degrees being handed out, and they do not equate to good paying jobs. Consequently, not only do parents go into debt, but also students incur heavy loan repayment after they graduate, and then in many instances find themselves unable to find a job to pay for it, or, they take a job outside their educational field in order to make ends meet.

Estimates of a college education average $47,000.00 a year for private colleges, and $24,000.00 per year for public colleges (based on in-state rates). More expensive schools can cost one-third more. My feeling is that college costs should not be rising faster than the normal inflation rate, but that has not been the case for many years now, with tuition costs spiraling ever upwards. If you think of an investment as an outlay of money for an expected profit, college could provide both monetary, social and intellectual benefits. The operative word is "could." Regarding a return on money spent, if you can't get a job when you graduate that fits your higher education skills, or you end up taking a job outside of your chosen field at compensation similar to other jobs held by high school graduates, then what have you gained? The social benefits can be gained from life experiences without the cost. Finally, intellectual benefits can also be gained in many ways for those with a thirst for knowledge, and also for little cost.

As if the cost was not a big consideration, we also have to look at student statistics. According to the National Center for Education Statistics (www.nces.edu.gov), only 83% of high school kids graduate, and a four-year degree graduation diploma is only awarded to 59% of all college students (62% female, and 56% male).

In thinking about these odds in a different manner, a better way might be to have your son, or daughter, sit for the S.A.T. examination, and then use the results to apply for college. Then, with the college acceptance letter, they could then attach those documents to a resume' and apply for a good paying job. Most employers would clearly see that the job applicant knows how to think, enjoys reasonably good intelligence, and therefore can be trained to the employer's method of doing business. In this way, instead of having a huge student debt load at the end of four-years (upwards of $250,000.00 for a quality university, and with graduate school, it could easily run into $400,000.00), your youngster would have four-years of pay-checks instead, with no debt! If, however, your youngster is not college material, then do everything you can to place them in a trade school, where they can gain skills that are needed in society, and that pay, in many cases, more than what many college grads are able to earn. Another fall-back position would be the military where they could obtain a free education and survival skills. Also, helping them start their own Business, is another option, if they have the maturity to do so. Any of these alternatives deserves some consideration.

Finally, if you do happen to have a really bright kid that excels in math and science, then perhaps you should explore the idea of college, because their chances of succeeding after graduation are far greater. According to USA Today (7.23.2017), Architecture, Physical Sciences, Business Finance, Communications, and Bio Sciences are the top majors in demand in our economy. I do understand that it is natural for parents to want their kids to go to college, but it should not be done so before making sure you have saved adequately for your own financial goals. There are two reasons for this, neither of which is selfish. First, the college financial-aid system penalizes parents for saving money outside of their retirement accounts, and they can be penalized even more if the money has been invested in the youngster's name. The second reason is simple. You don't want to be depending on your children in your old age do you?

In hunting for college education funds, you should apply for student financial aid by completing the FAFSA application – www.fafsa.ed.gov. Some schools supplement FAFSA with the college board's CSS/financial aid PROFILE form. You should also visit the Federal Student Information Center while you are at it - www.studentaid.ed.gov. Many states also have their own student financial aid programs. Depending on your circumstances you may also wish to check out Custodial Accounts, 529 Plans, and Educational Savings Accounts (ESAs). Student loans can also be obtained from Stafford Loans (unsubsidized), and Parent Loans for Undergraduate Students (PLUS). There are also Grant Programs available through schools, state governments, the federal government through FAFSA, and other independent sources such as employers, credit unions, community groups, and non-profit foundations. The Coverdell Program (Peace Corp.,) is another opportunity. You should also check the data base at your local library, and visit your child's school counseling department for other options.

My approach in discussing the heavy cost of higher education, is meant to be both practical and philosophical, by asking you to think outside normal parameters when this topic comes up for family conversation. It is an expensive and serious decision to make, and I have simply wanted to provide you in this segment with some additional thoughts for your consideration. In reality, it's all about using good common sense, so that you can make the system work in your favor, rather than becoming a potential victim of it.

SUMMARY RECAP

Now that some of the higher expenditure costs have been explained, we need to recap and highlight what we have learned in this chapter. The steps involved in putting together a good family budget require some work and planning. However, once the budget is established, it becomes very easy then to track your income and expenses in a way that puts you in charge, and not the other way around. So here is a recap:

Step One: Each adult member of the family should track their daily spending for a complete month. Each person should have their own note book, and be expected to be held accountable for all money they spend. This is not used to pass judgment, but rather to create true spending patterns of how the household income is actually spent. Adjustments can always be made later.

Step Two: Simultaneous to tracking your daily spending habits, you can create a Balance Sheet by writing down all your asset values, and all your liabilities. This exercise will show you the big picture of where the household stands today at a particular moment in time. This completed Balance Sheet will be used to create your action plan later on. You will also be able to look back in the future with a sense of accomplishment in judging how far you have progressed.

Step Three: Use the average household spending categories as an anchor in preparing your own personal budget. This is a collaborative endeavor, where all the participating family members need to get involved. Remember, all household budgets are different, and you must adjust to accommodate the realities you are faced with. Also, budgets do change and need to be adjusted from time to time.

In each and every step in the process it is important to pray about your spending habits, and the plans you hope to accomplish for the future. Let go and let God get involved as a partner with you in the process. It is much easier knowing that God is part of the project. Why? Because you know you cannot fail with God steering the ship.

Are you beginning to feel like you are getting more in control of your money and spending habits? There is nothing more satisfying than knowing you have your family finances under control. Not only is it a great morale booster, it is also biblical. God has always recommended that we live within our means, and learn to be content with what we have.

THE IMPORTANCE OF A SAVINGS ACCOUNT

Under the personal budget heading of "Savings for goals," financial experts recommend a sum equal to 12% of your net monthly income, which you will find the true benefit of in a later chapter. After ensuring your tithing is paid, you need to make a habit of putting money consistently into savings. We need to learn from the little squirrels that save in the summer for the winter, in order to survive. Savings is a form of practice, which must be done consistently like changing any other old habit. So every time you pull out your credit card or wallet, ask yourself if you really need whatever it is you are thinking of buying. Often times, by delaying the decision until later, it does not appear to be such a want or a need after all. As you build your capital, you obtain a return on it, which can eventually allow you to survive independent of your job. Remember also that savings can lead to a far more enjoyable retirement.

You have now established your personal family budget by analyzing your spending habits and recognizing the differences between wants and needs, and emotional and impulse spending. You are now ready to tackle the next step in the program, which is to put a system in place that will get you out of debt once and for all, which is the subject of the next chapter.

BUDGET WORKSHEET	Daily Records	Adjustments	Month 1 Budget	Actual	Month 2 Budget	Actual	Month 3 Budget	Actual	Total
Charitable Giving									
Rent or Mortgage									
Second Mortgage									
Life/Health Ins.									
Home/Renters Ins.									
Auto Ins.									
Child Support									
Monthly Debt Obligations									
Savings for Goals									
Total Fixed Expenses									
Food for the Home									
Meals/Snacks at Work									
School Lunches									
Meals Out									
Electricity									
Gas/Heating									
Water/Sewage/Garbage									
Home Phone									
Smart Phone(s)									
Cable/Satellite									
Internet Charges									
Car Gasoline									
Bus Fares/Parking/Tolls									
Clothing									
Uniforms									
Dry Cleaning/Laundry									
Cleaning Supplies									
Grooming/Personal Items									
Kids Allowance									
Baby Sitting									
School/Tuition Activities									
Cigs/Tobacco/Alcohol									
Recreation									
Newspapers/Magazines									
Hobbies/Lessons									
Doctor Visits									
Dentist Visits									
Medicine									
Bank Charges									
Postage/Envelopes									
Total Variable Costs									
Back to School Items									
Car Repairs									
Auto Tags/Inspection									
Gifts – Holidays									
Appliance Repairs									
Home Maintenance									
Total Periodic Expenses									
TOTAL MONTHLY EXPENSE									
MONTHLY NET INCOME *									
SURPLUS OR NEGATIVE									

*This figure represents the total net family income after taxes from all sources
The Daily Records are the total sum collected over the last 30 days

Figure 5.4

CHAPTER SIX

DEBT AND THE DEVIL

The witness has forced himself to testify.
For the youth of today, for the children who will be
born tomorrow. He does not want his past
to be their future!

– Elie Wiesel (1928 – 2016)

WHILE GOD is consistently telling us to avoid debt, we find the devil doing just the exact opposite. The devil wants to make us slaves to debt so that he can create the torment, stress and anxiety he likes to inflict on so many unsuspecting people.

Since the genius of fractionalized banking was developed, there is no question that the next great revolutionary idea was the development of the powerful creation of compound interest, which is currently making obscene profits for lenders, and putting American families further and further into debt. Albert Einstein referred to compound interest as the greatest opportunity of the 20th century. This opportunity, however, is clearly for the lender and not the borrower. This point was expounded on further by J. Rueben Clark Jr. who stated:

> "Interest never sleeps or sickens nor dies. Once in debt, interest is your companion every minute of every day and night; you cannot shun it or slip away from it; it yields neither to entreaties, demands or orders; and whenever you get in its way or cross its course or fail to meet its demands, it crushes you."

It is very important to keep two things in mind concerning borrowing: 1) every time you borrow money you subtract from your future income, and 2) when you borrow, you immediately reduce your net worth position, except when you use a loan to purchase some asset of equal or greater value. To make my point even clearer, we have about 320 million people in America, which includes our kids. Yet, greedy, avaricious lenders mail out more than four billion credit card applications to American households each year, the vast majority unsolicited. Need I say more?

I will now provide you with a couple of case studies to further reinforce my point about debt, and then show you a method to get you out of debt once and for all.

CASE STUDY # 1:

Up until a few years ago, Mary Howard was a "dream borrower," according to the LA Times. She had an adjustable rate mortgage on her home (ARM), her auto loan, and five credit cards where she made minimum monthly payments on all obligations. The interest and fees she paid represented 40% of her $50,000.00 a year salary, or about $20,000.00 per year. With little savings to fall back on, she experienced a medical emergency, which caused her to lose her job.

Her debts then spun out of control, and eventually she lost her home and her financial position was ruined. There are many lessons to learn from this poor woman's circumstance, but the most important is to avoid debt and the poverty it causes. So, if you are already in debt, then getting out of it is priority number one, because until you do, you will never build wealth.

CASE STUDY # 2:

In this next case, the situation is nowhere near as dangerous as the first case was, but trouble could be on the horizon if this couple, Rex and Flo Alexander, don't start taking their finances more seriously. Below is how their debt picture looks:

Description	Monthly Payment	Interest Rate	Number of Payments Remaining	Remaining Debt	Total Debt
MasterCard	$ 55	18.0	9	$ 460	$ 495
Visa	$ 110	16.5	24	$ 2,236	$ 2,640
Dental	$ 215	12.0	12	$ 2,420	$ 2,580
Auto # 1	$ 220	12.0	32	$ 6,000	$ 7,040
Auto # 2	$ 325	9.5	16	$ 4,866	$ 5,200
Residence	$1,199	6.0	349	$197,544	$418,451
	$2,124			$213,526	$436,451

The above credit balances were prioritized by paying off the highest interest rates first, although in your case you may prioritize according to paying-off the smallest balances first in order to gain a sense of satisfaction that you are making progress towards your goal.

In the above case, if Rex and Flo continued to pay minimum monthly payments on their six credit obligations, they would pay $222,925.00 in interest charges, bringing their total debt to $436,451.00! This is twice as much as what they actually borrowed! Such is the power of compound interest. It always works in favor of the lender, and never the borrower. That is why it is important to reverse compound interest in your favor by first getting out of debt so that you can then begin to loan your money at interest, and benefit from compound interest in your favor.

If Rex and Flo continue to make minimal monthly payments on their obligations, they will be paying off debt for the next 29 years. In actuality it is worse than that, for they will continue to make purchases on credit, which will eventually cause their credit balances to rise to a level where they eventually max out their lines of credit. It is sobering to think that Rex and Flo will be slaves to debt for most of their remaining lives, even taking their credit obligations with them into retirement. However, there is a much better way, provided Rex and Flo are willing to discipline their attitude towards executing a plan that will pay-off their debts in less than 12 years, even in less than 10 years if they refinance to a lower rate than 6%, which is advisable.

DOUBLE DOWN DEBT REDUCTION METHOD

Rex and Flo are paying out $2,124.00 per month in credit payments. Using the Double Down method the total monthly amount of $2,124.00 does not change, but it is paid differently. This couple must first concentrate on paying-off the $460.00 MasterCard bill. This will be accomplished in nine-months unless they are able to obtain additional monies by selling off some assets, or finding other ways to increase their monthly income such as working some overtime, or finding some cost cutting in other areas of their budget. In my opinion they should make every attempt to pay-off the Mastercard as quickly as possible, even in the first month, so that they can then use the $55.00 payment by adding it to the Visa payment. This increases the Visa payment to $165.00. I will save you doing the math by pointing out that the $2,236.00 owed on the Visa will be paid off in 14 months. So far we have eliminated two of the debts, thus saving $165.00 ($1,980.00 per year), and we are only 14 months into the program. Now, we attack the third bill (I like the word "attack," as it sounds like a war against debt, which it is). The third bill is the dental bill for $2,420.00. But guess what? It was already paid-off after the 12th month. So now we have three bills closed out, and we can now use the three payments: $55.00, $110.00, and $215.00, a total of $380.00, which is now added to our regular car payment of $220.00, making a total new monthly payment of $600.00 per month against the auto debt. Remember also that during the same 14 months that we were paying down the three debts, we were also making the minimum monthly payment on auto # 1 of $220.00 per month. Therefore, the balance owed has been reduced to $2,920.00, which, based on the higher payment of $600.00 per month, will be paid-off in five-months. We are now roughly 19 months into the double-down debt reduction program, and we haven't even begun to fight. Remember, more debt reduction is always better than less, and for sure is always better than a maybe. So keep up the good work as it is only going to get better. Read on.

We now tackle paying-off auto # 2 with a monthly payment of $925.00 ($55 + $110 + $215 + $220 + $325). Here again, while we were paying off the first four bills, we were also making the minimum monthly payment on auto # 2 of $325.00. Therefore, at the 19 month mark, the balance is now down to guess what? ZERO! Why? Because there was only 16 payments remaining, and we are 22 months into the program. I explained the issue in a linear fashion so as not to make it too complicated. The fact of the matter is, however, that we are now completely out of debt with the exception of the house mortgage. Now this is where the really big pay-off begins to kick in. We are now going to start paying $2,124.00 each month towards paying off the mortgage prematurely. In fact, if Rex and Flo follow through on their commitment to this program, they will pay-off the house in less than ten-years. Imagine being debt free so quickly. It is one of the best feelings in the world when you finally have a mortgage burning party!

There is one issue that we have not discussed regarding the double down debt reduction program, and that is we are not to incur any further debts. Credit cards need to be frozen, and impulse buying needs to be curtailed. This is the sacrifice Rex and Flo need to make in order to become debt free. It is true that some expenses will arise causing money to be spent out of their budget, but it must be justified and controlled in order to stick to the main goal of getting completely out of debt. Therefore such new debt must be paid off monthly or it should not be incurred. Naturally any additional debts will extend the total time period to get completely out of debt, perhaps extending to a little over ten-years the total time to get completely out of debt rather than less than ten-years. So it is important never to take your "eye off the ball."

This is not the end of the story, however. To phrase it in the famous words of Sir Winston Churchill: "This is not the end. It is not even the beginning of the end. But perhaps it is the end of the beginning." Yes, I want you to think hard and long about what Rex and Flo have accomplished. They are now debt free, and own 100% of the equity in their home. Their net worth has risen considerably to well in excess of $200,000.00, and they now have more than $2,000.00 in extra money to invest each month. Notice I did not use the word "spend." Rex and Flo were 36 and 35 years of age when they started the Double Down Debt Program, and they are now in their middle forties with their whole life ahead of them to invest wisely for a solid retirement.

The story I have just illustrated can happen to you too, but it will take sacrifice and commitment to make it a reality. It will also take prayer in order to create the staying power needed to see the strategy through to the end. But with God as your partner, I am confident it will happen for you!

Remember that in all the steps Rex and Flo have executed so far, they continued to tithe consistently each month because they too had learned the power of giving back to God for all that God has done for them. Knowing that everything belongs to the Lord allowed Rex and Flo to pray daily about their spending habits realizing that they had a responsibility to be good stewards of God's assets. And by being good stewards, Rex and Flo knew that God would do His part. If you are still struggling with this concept, please read Romans 12:2 which says: "Do not conform any longer to the pattern of this world, but be transferred by the renewing of your mind. Then you will be able to attest and approve what God's will is – his good pleasing and perfect will." A careful study of the Beatitudes found in the Book of Matthew 5:1, is also a wonderful place to learn how to transform your mind according to the dictates of what God wants for us. The transforming of your heart also requires lots of praying to God for help, and He will deliver.

A DOLLAR SAVED IS A DOLLAR EARNED

To further reinforce my point about getting out of debt, I want to provide you with one more illustration of just how powerful $1,000.00 per year ($83.00 per month), in reduced spending, adds up to over a 40 year time period. Table 6:1 below assumes you invest this $1,000.00 in a tax-deferred retirement account with an average 8% rate of return on your money, and that you are in a combined 35% federal and state tax bracket.

For every $1,000.00 that you can reduce your annual spending you will have this much more money in your bank account instead of somewhere else.

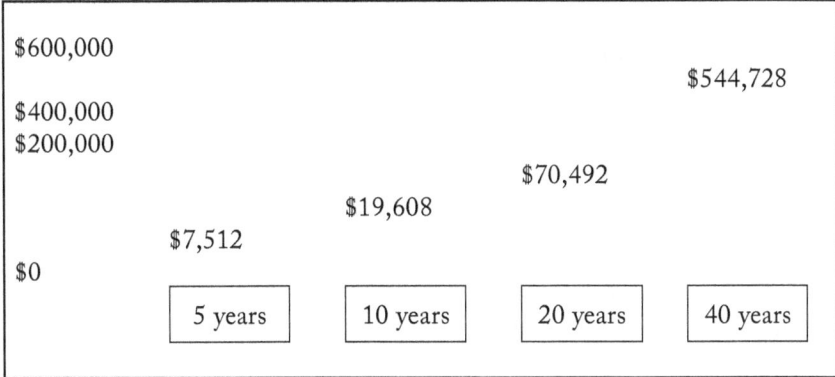

$600,000			$544,728
$400,000			
$200,000			
		$70,492	
	$19,608		
$7,512			
$0			
5 years	10 years	20 years	40 years

Source: John Wiley & Sons

Table 6:1

DEBT COLLECTION LAWS

If you are not being chased by bill collectors, you may wish to skip this section. However, the reality is that millions of American families are currently suffering with huge debt problems, and are being harassed by bill collectors who are making their lives miserable. As if the worry of meeting next month's financial obligations were not enough, they also have to contend with menacing phone calls, dunning letters in the mail, and someone calling them while at work.

Not only do debtors worry about losing their jobs, but their imagination often reflects on the embarrassment of other family members, friends, co-workers, or neighbors knowing about their money problems. Therefore, to allay their fears, I am going to provide some information that will empower them by knowing just exactly what bill collectors can and cannot do according to federal law. The purpose is not to help you shirk your responsibilities, but rather to erase the fear and panic that sometimes sets in when a person does not have a plan to get out of the terrible circumstances they find themselves in. Yes, there is a way out. Read on.

The Federal Trade Commission (FTC), is the nation's consumer protection agency, among other things. Their job is to enforce the Fair Debt Collection Practices Act (FDCPA), which prohibits debt collectors from using unfair, abusive, or deceptive practices to collect money from you. The FDCPA defines bill collectors who regularly attempt to collect debts owed by others. These collectors could include collection agencies, lawyers, or companies that buy delinquent debts from creditors for pennies on the dollar, and then attempt to collect the full amount plus interest and other charges as well.

ANSWERS TO TYPICAL QUESTIONS ABOUT FDCPA:

The Act does not cover business debt, only personal, family, and household debts. This may include monies you owe on credit card debt, medical bills, auto loans, or your house mortgage.

Can a Debt Collector Contact Me at Any time or Place?

Collectors cannot call you at inconvenient times, such as before 8am or after 9pm, unless you approve it. Collectors are not allowed to call you at work if they have been told orally or in writing you are not allowed to take calls at work.

Can I Stop a Bill Collector from Contacting Me?

When a debt collector first calls you, try to find out all you can about the debt to see if it is owed by you, or is it some type of snafu that has gotten you mixed up with someone else. If you determine the debt is not yours, and the debtor continues to contact you, then you need to write a letter to the collection company via certified mail, advising them not to contact you again. Be sure to keep a copy of the letter for your file. This should stop the contact with two exceptions.

The collector can let you know that there will be no further contact, or that they or the original creditor intend to take a specific action like filing a lawsuit. Your letter does not get rid of the debt if it is genuine, and the creditor can still sue you.

Can a Debt Collector Contact Anyone Else About My Debt?

A collector can contact other people, but only to find out your address, your home phone number, and where you work, but they generally can only do it once. Other than what I have just said, a collector is not permitted to discuss your debt with anyone other than you, your spouse, or your attorney if he or she is representing you.

What does the Debt Collector Have to Tell Me about the Debt?

You must receive from the collector a validation notice advising you how much you owe within five-days of contacting you. The name of the creditor is mentioned, and what you must do if the debt is not yours.

What Limits Does the FDCPA Impose on Bill Collectors?

Bill collectors are not allowed to harass you or third parties they contact. They are not allowed to use threats to harm you, or publish a list of names of those who refuse to pay their debts. They are allowed, however, to send the information to credit bureaus if it is valid. They are not allowed to use obscene language or repeatedly use the phone to annoy people. Furthermore, collectors cannot falsely claim that they are attorneys or government officials. They cannot pretend to be working for a credit bureau, and they cannot misrepresent the amount you owe. Also, they cannot indicate that papers they send you are legal documents if they are not, and they cannot advise you that legal documents are not legal if they actually are. They are not allowed to say that you will be arrested if you don't pay, or that they will garnish your wages or sell your property unless they are permitted by law to do so.

Can a Debt Collector Garnish My Bank Account or Wages?

Yes, if the debt is valid, but they must first obtain court approval, which requires a law-suit first. Keep in mind that such income as social security benefits, SSI, veteran benefits, civil service and federal retirement and disability benefits, military annuities and survivor benefits, are exempt from a garnishment attachment (which is generally a maximum of 25% of a person's weekly pay-check).

Do You Have Recourse Against a Bill Collector who Violates the Law?

Yes, you must sue within one-year either in a state or federal court. If you can prove damages, you could receive compensation due to illegal collection practices, lost wages, and medical bills. Even if you are unable to prove actual damages, the judge could award you $1,000.00, and reimbursement for your attorney fees. Groups of people can file a class action law-suit for up to $500,000.00, or one-percent of the collector's net worth, whichever is lower.

WHERE DO YOU FILE A COMPLAINT REPORT AGAINST A BILL COLLECTOR?

To file a complaint with the FTC, simply go on-line to: www.ftc.gov, or call: 877-382-4357.

UNFAIR BUSINESS PRACTICES:

Debt collectors are not allowed to engage in unfair business practices, like trying to collect interest and fees, separate from what you owe, unless the contract or state law allows the charge. They cannot deposit post-dated checks early, and interestingly enough, they cannot contact you by postcard.

Hopefully, this information should prove useful to all those stressed out families who are having problems with harassing creditors. Now that you are fully informed, you have leveled the playing field, and placed yourself on an equal footing with bill collectors. Once a collector realizes that you also know the law, and what your rights are, the conversation and the process should go much more smoothly for you.

A STORY OF INSPIRATION FOR US ALL

I would like to mention the story of my friend, Ray, who retired only to find out a number of years later that he and his wife had accumulated about $40,000.00 in revolving credit card debt. They had not made the adjustment in their new life-style retirement income to allow for less income coming into the household, which is a common mistake that many people make. As a consequence, bill collectors were hounding him. Advisors told Ray to simply take the easy way out by filing personal bankruptcy, but he refused. Instead of running from his problems he faced up to them like the good Christian man that he is. Although he knew his rights, he took a different type of action. Due to his strong character he felt obligated to pay all his debt, so he looked for and found a part-time job cleaning tables at McDonalds, which is where I first met him. He worked out pay-back plans with his creditors, and one day he told me his story to let me know that he was down to his last $10,000.00 owed, which he hoped would be fully paid-off by the end of 2017. Cleaning tables and toilets in your retirement is not exactly what most people want to do. But Ray, God bless his soul, did it the hard way. The interesting part of the story is that he came to enjoy his work, and made many friends, and in so doing, inspired a lot of people, including me. God works in mysterious ways!

By the way, Ray's story also highlights another very important point about debt. Believe it or not, the best investment you will ever make while you are in debt, is paying off your debt obligations. The interest you save will far exceed most other investments. So, until your debts are paid off, think twice about making other investments. A year or two from now you will be far better off financially if you concentrate on debt pay-off rather than trying to make much smaller returns on other investments. The only exception to this rule is to always put money to one side for emergency purposes.

Before wrapping up this chapter, I should point out that when you have a lot of debt, you will be approached by numerous debt management companies who will tell you how they can fix all your debt problems, whereby you are put on a repayment plan with your creditors, and the agency gets a monthly fee for managing the payments. These plans can be costly, and my recommendation is to avoid them like the plague. This book is providing you with an ample arsenal of knowledge for you to work out your repayment program by yourself, and keep the fees for yourself. If you want to educate yourself further you may wish to contact The Institute of Financial Literacy, a good agency that does not offer debt management programs. You will find them at: www.financiallit.org.

BUDGET AND DEBT TRACKING TOOLS

Creating a budget and debt tracking system to track your debt obligations is as simple as keeping written records in a log system, as mentioned earlier. However, for those of you who like using computer software, there are a number of software programs you can use to accomplish the same thing including: www.budgettracker.com, www.yodlee.com, www.wally.com, www.mint.com, www.Geezeo.com, and www.mint.com, to name a few. You might also want to check out www.quicken.com, but instead of using their checks (which are expensive), you may want to order checks from: www.checkstomorrow.com.

Now that you have a way out of your circumstances, it is now up to you to implement the debt reduction program with the help of your family, and God. Yes, there will be times when you fall short, but if you keep going to God in prayer, He will see you through to the very end. Trust me on this one. God will always be there with you if you will only let Him.

CHAPTER SEVEN

MAKING THE CREDIT SYSTEM WORK FOR YOU!

One generation creates; the next generation
dissipates; one generation earns, the next burns;
one generation composes, the next disposes!

– unknown

IT WASN'T ALWAYS like this, where average Americans are currently drowning in a sea of debt. In fact, our grandparents, who mainly paid cash for their needs, with the possible exception of their home, would be shocked to their very core if they were alive today to witness the craziness and desperation that goes on in so many households, where families are living as slaves to debt. In Grandpa's day, credit cards had not even been invented, and Madison Avenue had only just begun to advertise small household products on the screen of a new invention called the television.

Saving money and cursing the sins of debt was the theme back then. This point is clarified by looking below to see how our savings rate has dropped since Americans started using debt instruments to live their lives:

Decades	Net Savings as a Percentage of Net National Income
1960s	9.9%
1970s	8.6%
1980s	5.7%
1990s	4.8%
2000s	2.3%

Source: Bureau of Economic Analysis – www.bea.gov

It was about 1950 when Frank McNamara began pitching the idea of a Diners Club plastic card to use as a substitute for money when purchasing meals in New York City restaurants. It soon caught on, and that was the beginning of the credit card industry. I wonder what Mr. McNamara would be thinking today if he were still alive? A few years later, the Bank of America created their own plastic credit card, which later became Visa. Soon others joined the system, such as Sears with their introduction of the Discover Card. Since that time we have witnessed a huge increase in credit card transactions directly at the expense of cash. In circa 1970, only about 15% of Americans used credit cards, but today that percentage has rocketed up to 80%! Most Americans have at least one credit card, and the average credit card holder has about seven cards.

A PERSONAL STORY

Many years ago, when I arrived in Los Angeles as an immigrant, I found that the job I had counted on was acquired by someone else. Suddenly, I found myself in terrible circumstances. I had no job, no friends, no networking system, and only $150.00 in my pocket. I slept in my car to save money until I found a job. One night, as I sat in my car in downtown Los Angeles, I looked across the street to witness something I had never seen before. People were living in an abandoned parking lot sleeping under cardboard boxes and tents. They were all homeless. I vowed to myself there and then, that this would not happen to me. It was an epiphany that was burned onto the frontal lobes of my brain forever. I realized there and then, that in a capitalistic country like America, where you can pursue the American dream and prosper based on hard work and ambition, that it is also possible to become homeless. This was a different concept to the cradle to grave security system provided in England, where I came from. There are similar systems throughout Europe where most people intuitively know that the government is always there to take care of them if they fail.

Within a couple of years I was managing a consumer finance company where I made secured and unsecured loans to families and individuals. Customer credit in England, was nowhere as advanced as it was in America. Back then we called it the Hire Purchase System, whereby I and others would load up our large vans at the warehouse, then drive from customer to customer to sell all kinds of products, and to collect payments on a weekly basis, not monthly. So, quite frankly, I was shocked at the much higher amounts of credit obligations that our average American customers were responsible for, and the fact that they were allowed to make monthly payments through the mail. America was way ahead with their more sophisticated credit practices.

I often made family bill consolidation loans, which considerably lowered overall monthly payments, and relieved pressure on the family budget, only to find a year later they were back asking for more credit help. It was during this time that I gained great insights into the devastation and destruction that can come about when credit is abused, and not used wisely. I was saddened to see so many desperate families arguing over money issues caused by job losses, medical emergencies, or the husband or wife spending recklessly or charging on credit without thought as to how it was all going to be paid back. One customer refinanced his bill four different times over a two-year period to get cash out using the same reason each time, which was to pay funeral expenses for the death of his mother! Desperate people do desperate things. Some couples divorced, while others separated or went back to live with mom and dad. Others filed for personal bankruptcy, while some decided to skip town altogether and avoid facing the mountain of debt that they thought they could never repay. In looking back and comparing those experiences with present day circumstances, I can say that the only change is that personal consumer finance companies have been replaced by the credit card industry, and that the addiction to debt I witnessed with some families back in the late 1960's and early 1970's, when I was in that line of work, is actually more prevalent today due to the easier access to credit in general. It is also fair to say that indebtedness today is causing far more havoc to the average American household that at any time in our history.

UNETHICAL AND IMMORAL BUSINESS PRACTICES

As I mentioned earlier, I like to look at the big picture in assessing trends in business, and our economy in general. So when I read that banks and other lenders are mailing out more than four billion credit card applications each year, in order to solicit and hook Americans into accepting more and more debt, I get very perturbed. My anger increases when I read how these same credit card companies are targeting high school students to ensure that the next generation continues to play in this orgy of debt, just like their parents. The lenders are on to a very good thing, and they will do almost anything to keep the good times rolling. Bankers are even teaching our high school kids into believing that it is OK to put up to 20% of their purchases on a credit card. They are like wolves in sheep's clothing. They take the virtuous position that they are only trying to help our kids, but are secretly preparing them to think like their parents. Creditors know a secret that many people do not know, which is that when a customer gets into the habit of charging on a credit card for everyday ordinary expenses, they usually spend a lot more money. Some studies have demonstrated that credit card use causes the card user to increase their spending habits by up to one-third more than if they had paid cash for the same items. An excellent example was when McDonalds began to accept credit cards and saw their average sale increase from $4.75 to $7.00! That is a 47% increase, and the only thing that changed was the method of payment!

Total outstanding U.S. revolving debt in 2015, according to Creditcard.com was $937.9 billion, more than the GDP of Belgium and Denmark combined. This number has grown $100 billion since 2011. The average credit card interest being charged is 15%, and the average balance owed by American households, according to creditcards.com is $9,600.00. If a family are "revolvers" (explained below), paying, say $200.00 per month, it would take them 74 months to pay-off an average $9,600.00 balance. Total pay-back would be $14,800.00, including more than $5,000.00 in interest! This is money that should be in your bank account, and not the banks!

The reason given for such high amounts of credit balances, is the easy availability of credit. When someone offers the average person credit, it is difficult to say no. Unfortunately, all this aggressive and seductive credit card mail solicitation is ungodly, and is light years away from what the Bible has to say about such matters. Remember, when we open the Bible to learn about money management wisdom, we find God speaking to us. Is it not better to listen to God rather than a banker?

Credit card issuers divide the world into two groups. The first group is called "transactors," who use their credit cards for purchases, but then pay-off the balance each month thus incurring no interest charges. The second group is called "revolvers," who carry balances on their credit cards, thus paying interest charges every month. At the end of 2015, the statistics tell us that the number of "revolvers" accounted for 42.1% of card holders, and "transactors" accounted for 29.7%. The remaining 28.1% were dormant cards, where no transactions were made during that time period. No doubt "transactors" use credit wisely. They use credit cards for convenience and to earn points for air travel, vacations of other cash incentives. However, they never pay interest for these privileges. According to a Knight Ridder article, there are about 700 credit cards that offer perks, such as cash back, free gas or savings on a new car, and many of these cards are not charging an annual fee. Competition is tightening. If you are a "transactor" who has the sense to pay-off credit card balances each month, then the best places to shop for the very best credit cards are: www.bankrate.com, and www.cardratings.com, where you find about 11,000 staff written credit card reviews, which are helpful in pointing out the pros and cons of each card.

"Revolvers," on the other hand, take advantage of being able to own multiple credit cards, and charge on all of them. For "revolvers" it has been determined that for every 10% increase in credit, there follows a 1.3% increase in debt within one quarter, and a 9.99% increase in debt over the long term.

The addiction to credit card use begins early when our young people are not making a lot of money. Credit provides funds that otherwise might not be available. It allows our young, especially when they leave home, to live the life-style they have always been used to when living with their parents. Soon, they are driving around in fancy cars, dress well, and live in luxury apartments that all give the impression that they are affluent. Unfortunately, there is no substance underneath it all. It is an artificial life-style that will not last in the long run.

It is at this point that a cautionary statement be made to all parents. Proverbs 22:7 says: "The rich rule over the poor, and the borrower is the slave to the lender." The Bible goes on to point out that it is not a good idea to co-sign for someone else, irrespective of who it is (your kids for example). (Proverbs 17:18). A recent FTC study found that 50% of those people who co-signed for bank loans ended up making the payments themselves. Also, the same report mentioned that co-signing for a finance company loan upped the default rate by the borrower to 75%, which had to be paid back by the co-signer. I find it fascinating to see how ancient Bible money management principles are just as valid today as they were thousands of years ago when God had them written down for all ages to come. It seems like man's ego is always getting in the way, in that he thinks he is wiser than God.

THE FICO CREDIT SCORING SYSTEM

Two very bright men, Bill Fair, an engineer, and Earl Isaac, a mathematician, invented the Fair Isaac Credit Scoring System in San Jose, California. Today the system is known as FICO. Unlike my experience as a young consumer loan manager, where I personally made all loan decisions subjectively based on my assessment of the risk in each credit application, today we now find that more than 90% of all consumer credit decisions are being made by computers, not humans. There is no place for compassion or special extenuating circumstances in the decision making. You either qualify or you do not.

Most people don't realize that they have a number of credit scores, including FICO. The three major credit reporting agencies: Trans Union, Equifax and Experian use Vantage Scores, which is similar to FICO. Other scoring agencies include: CreditKarma.com, Quizzle.com, and Credit.com. FICO, however, controls 90% of all credit decisions, and is the dominant player in the credit game. So how does the FICO system work? Actually, most people don't really know. It's like trying to get access to the formula for Coca-Cola – it's a well guarded trade secret. We do know some things, however, which are the percentages FICO applies to five credit and debt categories. Here is the breakdown of the percentages:

35%	based on your credit history (your debt record)
30%	based on your loan and credit card debt (another debt calculation)
15%	based on the length of your credit history (how long you've been in debt)
10%	based on the types of credit (types of debt)
10%	based on new credit (new debt)

Notice how I inserted parenthetical statements after each line item? I did this to demonstrate that each of the calculations is based on debt criterion. In other words, the whole FICO scoring system is based on debt obligations. The question I like to ask is, where does income, savings accounts, real estate ownership and equity position, and investments in stocks and mutual funds enter the picture? It does not. This point exemplifies the fact that FICO is all about a borrower's attitude towards debt. Even if you had $3,000,000.00 in net worth, FICO would not take it into consideration in evaluating your FICO score. I find this amazing!

Let me illustrate my point further by telling you about a friend of mine who was fully supporting his daughter while she was away at college. She worked part-time and had two credit cards, which she paid off monthly, but she depended on dad for everything else. One day my friend found out that his daughter's FICO score was higher than his, yet he owned his own home, and was the owner of seven rental properties all producing good positive cash flow. He paid his bills in full every month, just like his daughter, and he had a seven figure net worth, yet his FICO credit score was lower. So who was the greater credit risk? The answer is obvious. Most people are fascinated when I tell this story.

Obviously, a good FICO score helps you obtain lower interest rates on debt, but it is not about winning the financial game. So don't buy into the con that debt is good for my FICO score, and the higher my FICO score the better I must be doing. What you should be asking is whether the debt is good in advancing you towards your financial goals. Rex and Flo Alexander's FICO score would probably have gone down after they completed their double down debt reduction program, because they no longer had any debt upon which FICO could rate them. Yet it is obvious to all that the Alexander's are a much better credit risk after they had completed the program. Despite the flaws I have mentioned in the FICO system, the vast majority of the bankers in the country rely on FICO scores to determine credit risk and how much of a credit limit to extend.

FICO CREDIT SCORING SYSTEM

The FICO credit scoring system assigns each consumer of credit with a score that ranges from 300 up to 850 points. The lower your number, the higher the rates of interest you are charged by lenders, for such purchases as automobiles and home mortgages. Here is the breakdown:

Excellent credit risk	760 +
Good credit risk	700 – 759
Fair credit risk	621 – 699
Poor risk	620 and below

Note that when dealing with banks and mortgage companies to obtain lines of credit, home equity loans, new home financing, or refinancing your existing home, they apply a debt to income ratio, which they like to see kept at 35% of your income or less. Simply add up all your outstanding monthly fixed debt payments, and divide by your net monthly income.

DELINQUENCY RATES BY FICO SCORE

Have you ever wondered how the credit system works in favor of creditors? The FICO scoring system, as mentioned, is based on how a customer responds to their debt obligations. The FICO score is based on the higher your FICO score the lower your predicted likelihood of defaulting on a credit obligation will be. The median FICO score is around 720, so you generally qualify for the best interest rates if your FICO score is in the mid 750s or better. Here is a chart from Fair Isaac Corporation that shows what the likelihood of delinquency is going to be based on a person's FICO score:

100%							
80% --83%--							
60%	70%						
40%		51%					
20%			31%				
				14%	5%	2%	1%
0%							
Up to 499	500-549	550-599	600-649	650-699	700-749	750-799	800+

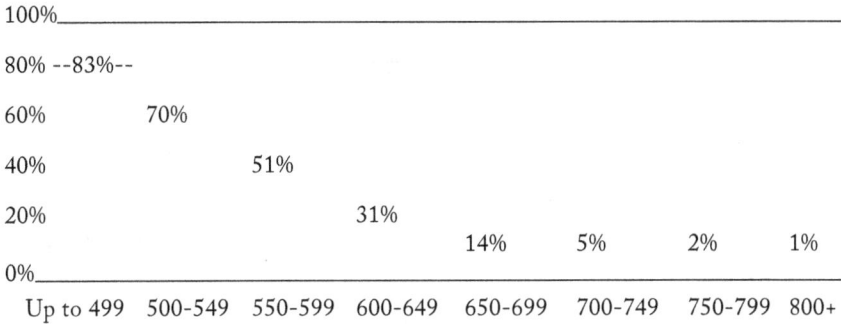

Before requesting additional credit, it is wise to calculate what your new monthly payment is going to be, and then check to see if it changes your debt to income ratio. If, for instance, it jumps up above 35%, you may think about paying off a bill to reduce your DTI, and then perhaps qualify for a lower interest rate on the new credit you are trying to obtain.

Most people don't realize that if they miss a car or credit card payment, their FICO score could drop 70 – 90 points. If a mortgage payment is missed, a FICO score could drop more than 100 points! A practical example is the purchase of an automobile for $20,000.00 financed over 60 months. The difference in interest paid between a person with a high FICO score versus someone with poor credit, can often be $5,000.00 or more! That is like throwing money down the toilet.

GUIDELINES FOR MAINTAINING GOOD CREDIT

1. Always pay your bills on time by setting up an automatic payment method on-line.

2. Keep your balances low. Use no more than about 30% of your credit limit.

3. Pay the balance off each month to avoid interest charges.

4. Avoid applying for too many credit cards.

5. Keep long standing accounts open. Length of history matters.

6. Review your annual free credit report (see below).

7. Assess your own credit worthiness by using the 5 Cs of credit:

   a. <u>Credit History:</u> Frequently review your credit history to ensure accuracy.

   b. <u>Capacity:</u> Always know your own DTI (Debt to Income Ratio).

   c. <u>Collateral:</u> Secured loans require collateral as a second method of collection.

   d. <u>Capital:</u> Review all your assets: savings, investments etc.

   e. <u>Conditions:</u> Be clear as to how you intend to use what you borrow.

HELPFUL POINTERS FOR FIRST TIME CREDIT USERS

I have spent a lot of time imploring you to get out of debt, if applicable, and only use the credit system if you intend to pay-off credit card balances each month. There is no question, however, that young people need access to credit simply for the convenience, and later when they get married and purchase their first home. So here are a few tips to get your credit established:

1. Pay your phone bill and utility bills on time.

2. Open a bank checking account and use a debit card to pay for everyday items.

3. Start building a savings account.

4. Get a secured credit card in your name.

5. Consider getting a credit card from a gas station or retailer, which are easier to obtain.

6. Get a student or auto loan in your name.

7. Become an authorized user on a trusted person's account.

Do yourself and your parents a big favor. Do not ask them to co-sign for you!

REPAIRING YOUR BAD CREDIT

If you have managed to obtain credit, but later experience a job loss, high medical expenses etc., which causes you to become delinquent, it will no doubt all show up on your credit report. Later, when you re-establish yourself, you need to clean up your credit as quickly as possible. You can accomplish this by writing an open letter to the credit reporting agencies explaining what happened, why it happened, and what steps you have taken to ensure it does not happen again. The letter is limited to 100 words or less – no long essays please. Be sure also to ignore solicitations from credit repair companies that promise you the moon in clearing up your credit, but generally do nothing more than what you can do for yourself. Save your money.

If you have a genuine complaint, and the creditor is unwilling to act to resolve the matter, you can file your complaint with the Consumer Financial Protection Bureau – 855.411.2372. Their website is: www.consumerfinance.gov.

REVIEWING YOUR CREDIT REPORT

Just like maintenance on your car, you should obtain a copy of your credit report at least twice a year to ensure everything is correct. If there are incorrect charges, you have the opportunity to clean them up before you apply for any major credit purchases. You can obtain a free credit report from www.annualcreditreport.com, or call them at: 877-322-8228. When you receive the report you will immediately notice that there is no credit score, because the 2003 law that mandates consumers being allowed to receive one free credit report each year, did not mention a credit score requirement, so it has been left out of the law. So, to obtain a credit score it will cost you. You could order from Fair Isaac, but they will charge you $19.95 for each of three credit reporting agencies (Equifax, Trans Union and Experian). For $29.95 you can obtain credit scores and reports from all three agencies at: www.truecredit.com, a division of Trans Union.

PAYING OFF CREDIT CARD DEBT

Here is one final reminder to reinforce the importance of the benefits gained by paying off credit card debt each month:

1. You save a lot of interest charges, which would have come out of future income.
2. You increase your free cash flow, which provides more flexibility in how you plan.
3. You improve your FICO score, qualifying for lower interest rates on cars and mortgages.
4. Your debt ratio becomes lower, making you a better risk.
5. Most importantly, you are now in a position to give more.

CREDIT SUMMARY

Large numbers of American families abuse their credit services as evidenced by the numbers. This is not a judgmental call, but only mentioned to point out that a lack of education about the wise use of credit is at the very heart of the problem. As an exercise, why not take the credit quiz at: www.creditcardquiz.org? You can then become your own judge of your credit knowledge.

Hopefully, this chapter has informed you to go forward with a different attitude towards using credit so that you become a "transactor" and not a "revolver." You want to use your credit privileges in smart ways to help you get ahead with your retirement program, or whatever other goals you may have for your family. When you are given a credit line from your creditor, it is like being given an alter-ego. With only $500.00 in the bank you now have credit access to perhaps $5,000.00, which boosts your spending capacity ten times. Whatever you do, don't allow this seductive temptation to cause you to fall for the trap. Don't be like the drug addict or alcoholic who suddenly comes into more cash to buy more of the same. Hopefully, the lessons I have mentioned throughout this book should have put that boogeyman away for good! By daily prayer, and letting go and letting God, you allow God to enter your financial decision making, which is one of the most important things you can do.

SECTION THREE

THE PROS AND CONS OF BUSINESS OWNERSHIP

(I must be bigger than my giants, or I will never overcome them, because my giants will always be bigger than me. I have to get out of my comfort zone, in order to grow!)

CHAPTER EIGHT

BENEFITS OF OWNING YOUR OWN BUSINESS

The thing that separates successful people from
those who are not, is not strength, it is knowledge;
it is not intellect, but persistence
and determination!

– unknown

BEFORE I GET into the benefits of owning your own business, which are numerous, I first want to point out that if you have absolutely no interest in pursuing business ownership, you may wish to skip the next three chapters. I do, however, recommend you read them, if for no other reason than the education you will gain, which can still save you a great deal of money in better understanding business and taxes in general. I also want to mention that if you already have a good paying job with benefits, you want to be sure you take advantage of all the perks your employer offers before contemplating business ownership. Therefore, before you think about anything else (starting or buying a business, or visiting a financial advisor, for instance), I want you to go through a little exercise to make sure you are getting everything you are entitled to from your employer, and at the same time ensuring you have developed a full appreciation for what you are getting. This is important.

The employment benefits being offered could include a 401K Plan where you can save up to $18,000.00 a year (2016), through payroll deductions, and if you are over 50, you can save up to $24,000.00 per year. Some employers participate by adding money to the plan for you. I should also say that your contributions are excluded from your reportable income, therefore paying no federal or state taxes, although they are subject to Social Security and Medicare taxes. Taxes are paid later after turning 591/2 or when you retire. 403(b) and 457 Plans are also available to employees of non-profit, or state and local governments. Also available, are medical, dental, and vision benefits for your whole family, often included at a considerable discount via the open market. Other benefits could include a yearly vacation, paid sick leave, maternity leave, fitness incentives, day-care for children, and tuition reimbursement. You may be able to buy your company stock at a discount, and obtain commuter reimbursement for those who take public transportation to work or pay parking fees. Also, let us not forget certain free legal services, and miscellaneous expense reimbursements, to name a few more. When you think hard and long about such benefits, it is easier to see that you are receiving far more from your employer than the net paycheck you take home. Your job not only provides steady income, but employers have plans in-place to help their workers enjoy a dignified retirement when they leave the company. Capitalism thrives on competition, and causes companies to offer such benefits, so that valuable employees don't move to another firm. Therefore, be sure to speak with human resources personnel to acquaint yourself with all benefits available to you.

On the other hand, you may not have a good paying job, or the education allowing you to get one. Therefore, the differential between what you make on your job annually, versus good paying jobs, can be considerable. It can often be the difference between renting versus owning a home, driving a good car versus an old junker, saving for retirement rather than depending totally on Social Security, and maybe working beyond retirement age to make ends meet. It is also the difference between paying minimum monthly payments on credit cards instead of paying off the balance. Insufficient household income can create a death spiral where people go further into debt in order to hold on to a particular lifestyle that they probably cannot afford.

BENEFITS OF OWNING A SMALL BUSINESS

I previously showed you proven methods to get out of debt and how to work a family budget. I also briefly mentioned a way of accelerating the process by also trying to increase your monthly income by working overtime, taking a second job, putting other members of the family to work, taking night classes to improve your education level, or selling off any assets that are not essential. What I did not mention, because I wanted to devote a whole chapter to the subject, is the tremendous benefits of owning your own business. Why? The reasons are many, which I will soon mention. Let me simply say at the outset that taxes are the biggest expense in America. If you add up all the taxes Americans pay annually, such as federal, state, social security, sales, gasoline, and other taxes, they are almost equivalent to the amount we all pay for shelter, food, clothing and transportation combined! Therefore, if we don't do everything within our means to reduce our taxes to the legal minimum, then shame on us! It will be difficult to achieve any serious wealth without tax planning. Someone once said that a taxpayer is someone who doesn't have to take a civil service examination to work for the government! How true!

Owning your own business in America today, is in my opinion the last great opportunity (especially for all those people who do not have higher education, or access to a good paying job), to rapidly increase their wealth, and pursue the American dream with gusto! Based on my own personal experience, business ownership is the fastest way in America to get rich. It is one of the last great options available to the average person. This explains why, according to *Entrepreneur Magazine*, more than 90% of home-based businesses make an average of over $50,000.00 per year!

Let's take a big picture view of business ownership in America. The numbers may startle you. There are 23 million small business owners who account for a whopping 54% of all US sales. Small businesses create 55% of all jobs (it is not the large Fortune 500 companies), and small businesses are credited with the creation of 66% of all new jobs since the 1970s according to the Small Business Administration. There are 600,000 small business franchises across the country, and they account for 40% of all retail sales, and provide jobs for eight million people. Small businesses also occupy between 30% and 50% of all commercial real estate space, which is an estimated 20 to 34 billion square feet! Small business loans surpassed $19 billion in 2014! These are very impressive numbers, and represent the backbone of the American economy. You will not find statistics like this when you travel abroad, where the ability for the common man to get ahead in business is far more restricted by large, inter-generational family combines.

A PERSONAL STORY

During my long business career, I have been blessed with a wide variety of business experiences including making thousands of consumer loans to family households, as well as being responsible for the shipment of more than $400 million in steel shipments per year, both domestically and in many foreign countries when I worked in Los Angeles. I have also been in business for myself for 30 years where I appraised and sold more than 250 small to medium sized businesses as a professional business broker. Consequently, I have witnessed with my own eyes numerous individuals who have accelerated their wealth position by starting or purchasing a business and going on to be millionaires. Unlike many other countries around the world, we Americans have great opportunities to start our own business from home or a commercial location. We can purchase existing businesses, often with the seller carrying back much of the selling price secured by the business assets; we can purchase new or existing franchise businesses. Finally, we can purchase pre-packaged businesses, known as Business Opportunities, for a much smaller cost, that have been successful in other locations across the country. In other words, it's a proven business-in-a-box ready to put together in your locality. Jobs come with annual pay increase caps no matter how good a job you do. This is not the case with business ownership, because there is no income ceiling caps. The sky is the limit. Small business ownership has no racial, age, or gender gaps. Everyone is equal in a meritocracy of going for the gold! It's all up to the individual! Even the disabled have started successful businesses from their homes. But before you consider venturing into you own business, you need to consider what God wants for your life, and you need to read the rest of this chapter.

Americans have several choices in earning income to survive. They can work as an employee and collect a W-2 form for tax purposes, which is what a high percentage of the population do.

They can work as free-lance independent contractors, paying their own taxes on an I.R.S. 1099 form, such as a real estate agent, for instance. Or they can start and grow their own real business.

If you choose to be a W-2 employee you get certain tax write-offs such as your IRA, and 401K contributions, as well as interest and property taxes on your home. You also get to write-off charitable giving. As a self-employed person you get to write-off all of the above items, but also a lot more. You can write-off your spouse and children (if you hire them), business vacations, medical expenses, cars, business meals, and even start a self-employed pension plan, which is one of the best tax write-offs of all. Home based businesses can also write-off a portion of the home.

Yes, it is a fact that you will never get ahead financially until you start a plan to reduce taxes to the bear, legal minimum, because tax savings can be used to pay down debt or be invested for your future. It is amazing how some people will spend hours fighting over some credit card charge of less than $50.00, but spend zero time educating themselves on taxes and other ways to increase their annual income by thousands of dollars of tax savings. So don't sweat the small stuff! Why chase pennies down the alley when you can collect dollars rolling down the street?

Federal Income Tax Brackets and Rates (2016)

Single Taxable Income	Married – Filing Jointly Taxable Income	Federal Tax Rate (Bracket)
$ zero $ 9,275	$ zero - $ 18,550	10%
$ 9,275 - $ 37,650	$ 18,550 - $ 75,300	15%
$ 37,650 - $ 91,150	$ 75,300 - $151,900	25%
$ 91,150 - $190,150	$151,900 - $231,450	28%
$190,150 - $413,350	$231,450 - $413,350	33%
$413,350 - $415,050	$413,350 - $466,950	35%
$ above $415,050	$ above $466,950	39.6%

Table 8-1

The above numbers help to demonstrate the reality of our regressive tax system, whereby we are penalized for earning more! Therefore, good tax planning should cause you to use every legal tax deductible expense possible in order to get into the lowest tax bracket, and save money. Educating yourself on taxes can be a big wealth saver when spread over a lifetime, so please take this point seriously.

SAMPLE CASE STUDY

The easiest way to demonstrate the power of a home based business ownership, is to show you the example of Lyle and Patty Jo Bernstein. Lyle earned $40,000.00 a year, or $3,400.00 a month, and there was always plenty of days left at the end of the month, long after they had run out of money. So his wife, Patty Jo, took a job working in a department store for $20,000.00 a year. Believe it or not, after adding up all her new expenses, she actually earned less than $1,000.00 for all her trouble! Here is why:

Gross annual income		$20,000.00
Less:		
federal and state taxes	$4,845.00	
Social Security at 7.65%	$1,530.00	
Travel to work = 10 miles round trip	$1,350.00	
Child Care (after credit)	$6,250.00	
Lunches at work - $7/day – 5 days a week	$1,750.00	
Business clothes / Dry Cleaning costs	$1,287.00	
Higher food costs (more eating out)	$2,000.00	$19,012.00
Actual Net Take-Home Pay		$ 988.00 (wow!)

Now, let's assume that Patty Jo started a home-based business. She would pay a lot less in taxes, and many of her expenses would be reduced or disappear. Why? Because she would be re-directing some of the expenses to her business as legitimate tax deductible items. Furthermore, we have not mentioned other life-style benefits, such as spending more time with the family, being her own boss and dictating her own hours, to say nothing of the greater freedom and satisfaction she enjoys in building her own business.

> **Disclaimer: Please note that as the author I have wide experience in business, but I am not licensed to give advice in medicine, accounting, taxes or law. I have no investments in insurance, mutual funds, stocks or bonds to sell you, and I am not currently licensed to sell securities or real estate, so I could not sell them to you even if you wanted me to. I have no ulterior motive other than a desire to help and assist you in gaining control over your financial life, and bring you closer to God's way of how you should manage money, if you are not already doing so. Before taking any action, I recommend you seek the assistance of your own professional counsel with regards to any information provided in this book.**

When you look at the above example, is it any surprise that millions of Americans own a small business working from home? Our economy has experienced a multi-fold explosion in self-employment during the last ten-years, and is likely to grow at a double-digit rate for the foreseeable future. Compare this with big business where growth and profits have dropped, and long term job security for young people has become a thing of the past. It is difficult to feel secure about your job when you hear about all the downsizing, rightsizing and capsizing that has become common in corporate America (department stores like Sears, Macy's and J.C. Penney, are, as of this writing, in serious financial trouble and pulling out as anchor tenants in many malls across the country. These companies have been staples in our economy dating back to the late 19th and early 20th century). As a consequence of all these seismic economic changes, employees are working for less, and seeking second jobs to make ends meet. A family with one job earner is becoming more of a rarity. Self-employment is certainly one good way to counteract these chilling trends.

SELF-EMPLOYMENT TEST

To be sure, not everyone is suited for self-employment, and a lot of time and money can be lost if one pursues business ownership without first ensuring they are compatible with the idea of being the boss of their own small company. Self-evaluation is the first item on the agenda, and at the back of the book you will find a number of questions that you should try to answer as honestly as possible. This may save you trouble later on. See Exhibit "A."

ADVANTAGES OF A HOME-BASED BUSINESS

In order not to lose focus on my primary purpose for writing this book, which is to get you to stop thinking like a laborer and get you to start thinking like a capitalist, by changing you from a slave to debt into a sharp investor with a great future ahead of you, I am limiting my discussion on self-employment to home-based businesses, and save the purchasing of existing businesses for another book.

As a retired professional business broker who has sold businesses in four states over a 30 year period, I have often been asked what is the best business to own? I like to joke (tongue in cheek), that the best business is one where I control the business check book, with no employees, no inventory, no accounts receivable, and no commercial lease responsibilities. In other words, keep it as simple as possible. "What kind of business would that be?" they would ask. My response was to do what I did - become a professional business broker where you contract to sell someone else's business, with an understanding that when it sells you receive upwards of 12% of the selling price, as a success fee, and in many cases much more. In reality, you temporarily become a junior partner in the Business until it sells.

I realize that not everyone wants to become a business broker, and if you already have a job, but it does not provide enough income for your lifestyle or future goals, then you may wish to hold onto the security of your job, and start a home-based business part-time, with the help of your family. Your overhead will be low at first because your rent or mortgage, utilities etc., have to be paid anyway. Therefore, you want to keep your break-even point at a bare minimum. What does break-even mean? Well, the best way to explain it, without going into a lot of accounting mumbo jumbo, is to provide a simple example:

A SIMPLE WAY TO DETERMINE YOUR BREAK-EVEN POINT

You decide to start a small business producing widgets, and you lease some commercial space at $1,500.00 per month. You determine your material costs to be $10.00, and you hire a person for $15.00 for each widget produced, which takes about one hour.

Step One: First, add up your fixed costs. These costs are inflexible and independent of sales volume. Such costs would include: rent, insurance, office supplies, maintenance, interest, and administrative costs. We figure the fixed monthly costs to be $2,500.00.

Step Two: Determine your variable costs. These costs vary with sales volume. In this case you have $10.00 for material costs and $15.00 in labor for a total cost of $25.00 to produce each widget.

Step Three: You decide to sell the widgets for $75.00, which gives you a $50.00 gross profit: $50.00 / $75.00 = 67% gross profit margin.

Step Four: You now divide your fixed costs by the gross profit margin. The answer will tell you how many widgets you need to sell in order to break-even on your costs. This is a point in the month where you neither make a profit nor incur a loss – you simply break-even. Any widgets sold above this number provide you a profit. Any number of widget sales below this break-even point means you are losing money.

BREAK-EVEN = $\dfrac{\text{Fixed Costs} \quad \$2,500.00}{\text{Gross Profit} \$ \quad 50.00}$ = 50 widgets sold to break-even

(50 widgets @ $75.00 = $3,750.00 sales)

So, in this case, you would need to sell 50 widgets per month or create $3,750.00 in sales in order to break-even on your total monthly costs. Now, if you decide to produce the widgets in your home garage, you would save $1,500.00 per month in rent, thus reducing your fixed costs down to $1,000.00. This would mean that you now only need to make and sell 20 widgets instead of 50 to break-even, or do $1,500.00 in sales per month. Further, if you got a family member to build the widgets, you could eliminate the $15.00 labor cost per widget, which would now result in you earning $65.00 on each widget sale, meaning you only have to produce and sell about 15 widgets to break-even, or just over $1,100.00 in sales. Working your break-even point is a handy way to quickly know where you stand at any time during the month. This exercise clearly provides you with the control you need, and allows you to play with different options of widgets sold to figure out where you need to be at any time in the month.

The above example is a manufacturing operation. However, if you are simply buying product from a warehouse, manufacturer or importing from overseas, then creating a break-even point is much simpler. All you do is figure out a reasonable gross profit margin that will cover your product costs and profit, and then divide this figure into your fixed costs. This will tell you how many products or gross sales you have to make each month, in order to reach your break-even point.

BUSINESS TAX WRITE-OFFS

The tax benefits you gain from owning your own small business requires much greater detail and explanation than I can provide in this chapter. All I am attempting to do is to provide you with enough information to whet your appetite to know more. With that said, I will now list, in an abbreviated form, a number of tax benefits that are readily available to most self-employed operators. The actual I.R.S. tax deduction list is much longer in scope:

BUSINESS TAX WRITE-OFFS

~Charity donations

~Home (a portion of it if you are home-based)

~Wife and children, if you hire them

~Car, and even a second car if your wife is involved

~Business meals

~Business vacations

~Medical plans

~Cell Phones

~Travel

~Kid's college education (if you plan it right by using their paycheck to fund it)

~Self-employed pension plan (a goldmine of tax savings)

~Gym costs, football tickets, country club dues

~All your normal business expenses: printing, advertising, brochures etc., and much more

Also keep in mind that Congress will subsidize your Business if you have a loss in the first year or so, by allowing you to deduct any losses against other income earned, such as your employee wages, your wife's employee wages (if you file jointly), dividends, earned interest, and pensions.

Even if the business loss exceeds the combined wages of you and your wife for the year, the government allows you to carry-back the loss for two-years and get a refund from the IRS for up to the last two-years of income taxes paid. Or you can carry-over the loss for 20 years. Yes, you can offset 20 years of income.

There are numerous, legitimate business tax write-offs in our tax code, over and above the write-offs allowed to W-2 employees. If you don't take advantage of many of them you end up leaving an awful lot of money on the table!

TYPES OF HOME-BASED BUSINESSES

By concentrating on the creation of a home-based business, it allows you to keep your present income flowing into the household, and at the same time minimizes the risks involved. This is due to the fact that a lot of your fixed overhead for the business has already been covered by your normal living expenses: mortgage, rent, utilities, insurance etc. At the back of the book I have listed a large number of small businesses that are compatible with being managed from your home. See Exhibit B.

STEPS TO CONSIDER IN LAUNCHING YOUR HOME-BASED BUSINESS

1. Try taking the self-employment test at the back of the book. Is it for you?
2. Figure out the type of businesses you see yourself managing.

3. Do you have enthusiasm, passion, and emotional attachment for your idea?

4. Can you use your education, hobbies, experience, and life skills to good advantage?

5. Apply synergy. Are there some natural resources that you can tap into?

6. Create a Business Plan (explained later), to answer all the hard questions.

7. Constantly apply creative thinking, and the power of positive thinking.

8. Should you or your spouse manage the business? Who keeps their job?

9. Can the kids and other family members get involved?

10. Thoroughly research your market and competition to assess your odds of success.

11. Test market your product or service to gauge receptivity.

12. Create a conservative financial projection for the first twelve-months.

13. Create a Break-Even Analysis to determine your minimum monthly sales.

14. Research your state licensing requirements, for compliance.

15. Do a review of any Home Owner Association restrictions.

16. Stay away from businesses that require frequent visits from trucks and customers.

17. Discuss your ideas with an accountant, business lawyer, and other trade sources.

18. Choose the best business entity for your needs (explained later).

19. Look into bookkeeping, taxes and insurance requirements.

20. Do a holistic test. Consider everyone's health and time commitments. Compatible?

In this chapter I have spent considerable time in explaining the many benefits of going into business for yourself. These benefits truly are amazing in building wealth. However, in discussing the many tax advantages, I would be remiss if I did not mention the fact that the IRS expects you to run your business like a business. The Hobby Statutes are on the books for a reason. If the IRS suspects you of using a hobby as a business for tax write-off benefits, then all your deductions could be forfeited, and you could be presented with a large, unexpected tax bill.

In the next two chapters I will summarize the benefits of using a Business Plan, and the advantages and disadvantages of business entities.

CHAPTER NINE

METHODS TO REDUCE
BUSINESS RISK

*We are continually faced with great opportunities,
brilliantly disguised as insoluble problems!*

– unknown

AT THIS POINT you may be seriously looking into the idea
of owning your own home based business, but perhaps you feel
you need further understanding concerning protecting your family from law-suits, and minimizing any liability that may be
involved. Please understand that all life is a risk, because it comes
with no minimum guarantees. We take a risk when we choose a
career, get married, have kids, and purchase our first home. At
every step there is risk because we don't know the future. Starting
your own business is also a risk, as some 23 million small business owners are aware. However, please keep in mind there are
many ways in which you can reduce risk to an acceptable level.
Think of the risk in making a business decision as a number
between zero and 10, with 10 being the highest level, and zero
being no risk at all. If, for example, you perceive the risk to be an
8, 9, or 10, then you would be foolish to take such a risk unless
you could find some way to reduce the risk down to say a 2 or
a 3, realizing of course, that you will never get to zero. All decisions have risk, so it becomes a question of analyzing the risk,

and then doing everything within your power to reduce it to its lowest common denominator to somewhere between zero and 3.

When you are put in a position of making a decision where risk is involved, you are well advised to take it first to the Lord in prayer, and ask Him to be your partner in the decision. Why? Well mainly because He knows the future, and He wants you to be successful if you are complying with the biblical points I have been making throughout this book. He knows the future, but you don't. So why would you not want to take on a partner as powerful as God, who can help you to squeeze most of the risk out of the situation? Sometimes God may think it is a bad idea, in which case He has done you a big favor by allowing you to hold on to your hard earned money. Secondly, you should always involve your spouse, and in some cases other family members in obtaining their opinion. Third, you should also seek out professional advice. You can talk to accountants, lawyers, business brokers, insurance brokers, manufacturer's representatives, and other third-parties that can contribute valuable information to you. By seeking out and using the experience of other helpful people, you can learn vicariously from their mistakes, and their successes.

With the above thoughts in mind, we will now take a look at ways to reduce your risk in going into business for yourself. We will first discuss the merits of a Business Plan. This is a critical exercise to conduct as it can prove invaluable to your ultimate success. Next we will look at forming the right business entity for you. Later, we will take a look at other ways to mitigate your risk through proper insurance coverage, and setting up trusts and pension plans.

YOUR BUSINESS PLAN

Business Planning software programs are readily available for less than $100.00, which will provide you with a step-by-step approach for easy completion. Some of them are listed in the back of the book. Here, I am simply going to point out some tried and proven techniques, and strategies, that you should keep in mind as you build your plan.

Remember that today's planning is tomorrow's future. You may be thinking that I don't need a business plan to manage a small business from my home, which is somewhat understandable until you realize the benefits:

1. Your business plan can become a powerful management tool, because it will cause you to ask all questions that are relevant to your success.

2. It can be used as an internal document to help you compare your results against goals.

3. It can be most helpful when working with other members of your team.

4. Finally, it can be used to gain outside financing if you have the need to do so, either now or later.

Business plans can range anywhere from five-pages up to thirty-pages, depending on the size and scope of the business operation. Mini Plans for small businesses, generally run five to ten pages, and contain most of the ingredients in a longer plan, but highlight the story instead. Presentation Plans, done with Power Point, usually show about 12 – 15 slides, when telling the story from concept to mission statement, and ending with your financial forecasts.

I remember the story of how Southwest Airlines, one of the most successful airlines in the country, came into being. Two men sat in a restaurant and wrote a triangle on a table napkin, which represented the map for their air route - Dallas, Houston, and San Antonio, Texas. Moral of the story – keep your plan straightforward and simple.

Writing the Business Plan

In writing the plan you will generally provide the following overview:

1. A Title Page
2. Table of Contents
3. Executive Summary
4. Management
5. Products and Services Sold
6. Industry Analysis
7. Marketing Plan
8. Financial Forecast

Some of the plan details should include:

1. **Your Business Concept**
   Discuss the industry you are in, your business structure, your products and services offered, and how you plan to make your business succeed.

2. **S.W.O.T.**
   Your plan should include the SWOT method (strengths, weaknesses, opportunities, and threats), which will provide you with a holistic, real life view of your business so that you can take all necessary steps to improve your plan.

3. **Your Strategy and Specific Action Plan**
   What are your goals, and how do you intend to accomplish them? When will you reach your goals?

4. **Your Products and Services**
   What are they, and what are their competitive advantages? This is your opportunity to really wow the reader by providing information that will explain why your customers will want to buy from you, and not your competition.

5. **The Market You Intend to Pursue**

   This is where you lay-out your marketing plan by answering questions such as: Who will your customers be? What is your demographic audience? How will you attract and retain your customers in a large enough volume to make a profit? What methods will you use to capture your audience? How will you set your products and services apart from your competition? Your unique selling advantages are crucial, and you should be able to articulate them in one or two clear paragraphs.

6. **Provide Antecedent Information on Your Management Team**

   Who will be managing the business? What is their background, and education level? What have they done? Describe their strengths and what talent they provide for your team.

7. **Financing Needs**

   This section provides several benefits. First, by doing a financial forecast, preferably for at least two-years, you force yourself to take a sober assessment of the forecast, and the reality of accomplishing your financial goals. Secondly, you can look at your forecast at any time during the time process to compare results with goals. Third, a written plan transfers thoughts and ideas in your head onto paper, thus providing another view of how this new venture, using your strategies and market assessments, will play out. Fourthly, if there are other team members, they can also benefit from being informed of what the boss is expecting to accomplish. Last but not least, you may want to use your business plan to promote outside financing to help the business grow faster. This will never happen unless you show a financial forecast that is solid. It is important to stick to the facts and not feelings; projections and not hopes, and realistic projections of profits rather than unrealistic dreams of wealth. Do this and you will boost your credibility considerably.

START YOUR SEARCH

Now that you have an idea of what goes into the creation of a business plan, and what questions need to be answered, you can now begin your search for valuable information. So here are a number of sources you can investigate to get the answers you are looking for:

Local Chamber of Commerce

Generally they will provide help whether you are a member or not.

Trade Shows

This is a great place to get lots of information on your specific products and services. You can talk to manufacturer representatives, and also find out what is "hot," and what is "not." Trade shows are invaluable in helping you determine the size of your market, your competition, and future trends. Start by going to: www.thetradeshowcalendar.com. This website will provide you with numerous trade show events going on across the country.

Business Magazines

You are certainly in the right country when it comes to magazines to help small business people. Here is a list that you may want to check-out:

Entrepreneur, Forbes, Fast Company, Small Business Trends, Small Business Today, Inc., Fortune, Businessweek, Business 2.0, Strategy+Business, Asia Inc., Latin Trade, Black Enterprise, Money, Money Management, Mashable, Success, Franchise Times, Tech Crunch, Wired, Harvard Business Review, Business 2 Community, EWeek, McKinsey Quarterly, Spice Business, Wall Street Accelerators, The Business, and a number of other regional magazines.

University Programs

Check out business colleges for incubator programs, and various small business support services.

S.C.O.R.E This acronym stands for Service Corps of Retired Executives, who donate their time for free to help people launch start-up enterprises.

State Commissioner of Economic Development

Many states support new business enterprises, and can often provide invaluable assistance in getting your business started, including free starter kits that provide all regulations, rules, and tax considerations.

Small Business Administration

This federal program provides loan guarantees to local and regional banks in order to increase lending services to local business. They also provide other business support programs.

ESTABLISHING AND CHOOSING YOUR BUSINESS ENTITY:

In this section we will discuss various business entities that you can form to suit the type of business you intend to manage, by taking into consideration taxes, liability issues, how much you can use in fringe benefits, and ease in raising capital from outside sources. The first and simplest to create is the Sole Proprietorship, which we will discuss first.

1. **THE SOLE PROPRIETORSHIP**

   This type of entity is the easiest to create and the easiest to close down. It's like camping. You pitch your tent, and when the vacation is over, you close the tent down and go home. Sole means one. You are the only person in the business, and because you have no employees, there are no IRS forms to file other than a Schedule C, which is an annual Profit & Loss Statement that is attached to your regular 1040 personal tax return to show profits or losses, which then adjusts your personal tax rate accordingly.

ADVANTAGES OF OWNING A SOLE PROPRIETORSHIP:

Low Start-Up Costs

Besides being very simple, your start-up costs are generally low. Without employees you have no filings with the federal government, no organizational documents to prepare, and there are no state filings unless you wish to use a name other than your own. We call this a Fictitious Name filing, which you record with your state for a nominal fee, of perhaps $10.00. The filing is generally good for about five-years and then it must be renewed. This prevents you keeping the name in perpetuity.

Direct Control

As the owner, you maintain maximum control of all aspects of the business at all times. You make your own decisions without having to get some partner to concur. In other words, if you make good decisions your risk should be very low.

Easy To Sell

Sole Proprietorships are the easiest business entity to sell, unlike corporations where there is a lot more involved.

Greater Tax Benefits

Unlike "S" corporations and partnerships (explained later), which have limitations; these same limitations do not apply to Sole Proprietorships. For instance, you are allowed to deduct your wife's salary, and deduct your medical expenses with a self-insured medical reimbursement plan.

Treatment of Losses

Any losses can be used to offset any other income you earn. Also, if losses exceed the current year's income, you can either carry back two-years, and offset the last two-years income, or carry forward up to 20 years, and use it to offset the next 20 years of income.

THE DISADVANTAGES OF OWNING A SOLE PROPRIETORSHIP:

Unlimited Liability

Unfortunately, the law classifies Sole Proprietorships as a type of alter-ego, in that the business is nothing more than an extension of you as an individual. This means that you are exposed to unlimited liability if the business is sued for any reason. Yes, you can take out liability insurance coverage, and take steps to mitigate your risk exposure. However, at the end of the day you have to do a reality check on what it is you do day in and day out. Some small businesses have very low risk due to the nature of what it does. An example would be a network marketing business where you act as a middle man to sell manufacturer's products. You keep no inventory because the manufacturer drop- ships the orders directly to your customers, and the manufacturer is held liable if there is a defect in the product. On the other hand, if you managed a home-based real estate business, you would be exposing yourself to high liability unless you obtained errors and omissions insurance. Even then, however, I would not recommend a sole Proprietorship for that type of business. Therefore, choosing a business model with low liability should be an important consideration, and many are presented in the back of this book for you to choose from. Taking out an umbrella insurance policy, which increases your insurance coverage, is another way to reduce risk, and the premiums are relatively inexpensive.

OTHER DISADVANTAGES

- It is much more difficult to raise capital with a Sole Proprietor.
- There is no continuity of the business life if the owner dies or becomes disabled.
- There is no check and balance system built in to the business model, such as a board of directors to advise the owner when he makes inadvisable decisions.

2. GENERAL PARTNERSHIPS

A classic partnership is where someone with know-how, but no money, partners with someone without know-how, but has money. Or, putting it a little more clearly, when a person with money meets someone with experience, the person with experience will get some money, and the person with money will get some experience!

There are two types of partnerships: General and Limited. We will look at both.

ADVANTAGES OF GENERAL PARTNERSHIPS:

Broader Management Expertise

Unlike a Sole Proprietor, who has to be good at doing everything within the operation, general partnerships have more people to divide up the work, which creates more efficiency, and provides greater knowledge to the business entity.

Easier to Raise Capital

There are generally no limits regarding how many investors can participate in a partnership. Because there are more people involved, there is generally more collateral that can be used for bank financing.

Easy Business to Form

There are very few filings with the I.R.S. or the states, unless you start hiring employees. All you need is a partnership agreement outlining the responsibilities of the partners. You should also enter into a buy-sell agreement that discusses what happens in the event of death or disability of a partner, or if one partner wishes to be bought out. Also, you will need to file IRS form 1065 – Return on Partnership Income, which makes the cost of filing a tax return a little more expensive than for a Sole Proprietorship. I should also mention that there is no double taxation because all profits flow through the partners onto their personal tax returns.

DISADVANTAGES OF GENERAL PARTNERSHIPS:

Money Draws

This can be a very contentious area for complaints among the partners, who often squabble over how much each partner gets in distribution of profits based on their performances. This is not a problem for a Sole Proprietor unless he likes to argue with himself.

Unlimited Liability

This type of entity is similar to a Sole Proprietorship in that each partner will experience unlimited liability unless there are specifically non-recourse debts, which means you have not personally guaranteed the debts.

Also remember that you are also personally liable for the action of your partners.

Other Considerations

It is very difficult to find the right partners who specialize in certain management areas, and often you will find partnerships dissolving because one partner is not pulling his own weight. Also, this type of entity has fewer fringe benefits than a corporation. You will find that the benefits from a self-insured medical plan are more limited for partners.

My experience over the last 30 years causes me to think twice about being involved in a General Partnership operation. I have witnessed partners fighting over money, power, and ego issues, and who are failing to perform their duties. It can be very sad and very expensive for everyone. In many instances, partnerships fail because there is no spiritual connection between the partners. When there is a spiritual connection, I have found a much higher level of trust between partners, and a much higher standard of integrity with every business decision made. So if you do decide to partner up with someone to start your own business, you would be wise to take it to God first.

3. LIMITED PARTNERSHIPS

This type of business entity was devised to provide limited protection for partners who invest, but who do not participate in the everyday managing of the Business.

ADVANTAGES OF LIMITED PARTNERSHIPS:

Limited Liability

One great advantage of being a limited partner is that you are only responsible for the amount invested, unless you personally guarantee a debt obligation. You are then shielded from all liability, unless you participate in the management of the operation. If you do later get involved in management decisions then you are considered an alter-ego of the partnership, and can be found liable. The general partner, on the other hand, is 100% liable for all obligations and liabilities of the entity.

MAIN DISADVANTAGES OF LIMITED PARTNERSHIPS

It is tough to sell a limited partnership interest, and in many cases the approval of the general partner is often required for any sale. Also, because the general partner is making the day-to-day decisions, you may ask who is checking on the general partner? An outside accountant may find out too late if there is an embezzlement issue.

So far we have covered the importance of business planning, and the benefits of creating a business entity, such as a Sole Proprietorship, General or Limited Partnership, in order to reduce your business risk, and turn the odds of success in your favor. Remember, the whole of life comes with risk, but that does not mean that you should be taking on unnecessary risk. The more we squeeze risk out of the equation, the better off we are. Also keep in mind that you will never reduce risk to zero, so don't fall prey to paralysis by analysis. At some point you must fire the bullet if you expect to hit bull's-eye!

After reading this chapter you may be thinking that there is a lot of work involved. Well there is if you try to do it all at the same time. However, by spreading the work-load over a period of time, you will eventually get to where you are ready to launch your business. Nothing happens without some effort, and there are a lot of people who have become millionaires by starting their own business. Take Harold Simmons, for instance, who grew up dirt poor in a shack with no electricity or plumbing. He is now worth $41 billion! Or, Shahid Khan, who came from Pakistan, and worked as a dishwasher for $1.20 per hour, and is now worth $3.8 billion! There are many self-made billionaires in America, and the number of millionaires who started with nothing is too numerous to count. The proof of which I speak is self-evident for anyone who wishes to do the research. With the right product, service, or unique idea, you can start a business and move up through the financial ranks faster than any other method out there. So, if you are not satisfied with your current income level, or time is flying by and you are not even close to achieving your retirement goals, then catapulting yourself forward with the profits of your own business is certainly worth looking into. There is one thing you can clearly count on - you are living in the best country in the world to make your business ownership dream come true!

In the next chapter we will discuss some other business entity types that you can take advantage of, depending on the type of business you will be creating. Always keep in mind, though, that your very best partner is the Lord Jesus Christ!

CHAPTER TEN

METHODS TO REDUCE
BUSINESS RISK – PART II

*A problem only exists if there is a difference
between what is actually happening, and
what you desire to be happening!*

– unknown

IN THE LAST chapter we covered ways of reducing your risk by executing a detailed business plan, and exploring the advantages and disadvantages of three business entity structures such as the Sole Proprietorship, the General Partnership, and the Limited Partnership. In this chapter we continue our discussion of business entity structures that include the general corporation, the "S" corporation, and the Limited Liability Company.

4. "C" CORPORATIONS

When you file for a corporation entity, you are automatically registering as a "C" corporation ("S" corporations will be discussed next). The dictionary defines a corporation as a legal entity that lives independently of the person or persons who have been granted the charter. The word "*incorporate,*" means to "create a separate body." This means that a corporation can outlive its owners (stockholders), enter into contracts, buy and sell assets, sue individuals and other business entities, and borrow funds. The business is owned by the corporation and not the individual(s) who formed it. This is an important point that many small business owners fail to grasp. So let's take a look at some of the advantages:

ADVANTAGES OF A "C" CORPORATE ENTITY:

Limited Liability

This is probably a corporation's greatest benefit. If it is set-up properly, and if the owners comply with corporate laws and formalities, then it can limit most liabilities to the assets of the corporation only, with the exception of fraud, malfeasance, malpractice, and non- compliance with corporate formalities that could cause a "piercing of the veil." This simply means that, under certain circumstances, creditors may penetrate the veil of corporate protection. Unlike general partnerships, if one of the corporate owners commits malpractice, then he would be the one libel, and not the rest of the investors. This is an important consideration.

Greater Tax Advantages

Regular "C" corporations and employees of "S" corporations who own less than 2% of the stock, get the most fringe benefits compared with the other entities. For example, you will get a 100% deduction for health insurance premiums for the corporate officers and their families; 100% deduction for disability insurance; 100% deduction for medical expenses that are not covered by insurance by using a self-insured medical reimbursement plan; tax free insurance up to $50,000.00 for term life policies, and qualified stock options that can provide capital gains. Also, corporations qualify for cafeteria plans that cover day care, adoption assistance, unreimbursed medical expenses, and legal advice.

Accumulation of Capital

Corporations are subject to their own set of tax rates, which allow the accumulation up to $50,000.00 of net earnings each year, taxed only at 15%. This allows corporations to build up capital for inventories, marketing programs, and other business expansion projects.

Other Advantages

It is easier to sell corporate stock without the need to obtain someone else's consent. Stock losses can be deducted up to $3,000.00 per year against other income, with a stock loss carry-forward benefit until the loss is satisfied.

CORPORATION DISADVANTAGES:

Double Taxation

Because a corporation is considered a separate entity, the owners are subject to double taxation. They pay tax on the corporate profits, and then again when they declare their corporate profits on their personal tax return. With proper planning, however, it is possible to avoid much of the double taxation by paying out bonuses and higher salaries.

Increased Administration Costs

Yes, there is more involved in managing your own corporation, including: yearly stockholder meetings to elect board members even if you are the only stockholder; corporate meetings must be kept; you need separate bank accounts, and keep very good business records. If you fail to do these things, your corporation may be classified as an alter-ego, and there goes the ball-game. You may then be liable for all corporate liabilities, including debts and other obligations. You also have to file a separate corporate tax return with form 1120. Also, as the employee of the corporation, you need to file with both the federal and state governments for an employment identification number SS-4, and an SS-5 for a Social Security card, as well as for unemployment.

Other Disadvantages

All losses with a corporation stay with the corporation, and can only be deducted against future income within the corporation. This means that corporate losses do not flow through to you on your own corporate tax return like they would if you were a partnership or Sole Proprietorship. It is possible to get around this issue, however, by filing an election for "S" corporate status, which we will discuss in a moment. As a small home-based corporate business, this next point will probably not apply to you, but is worth mentioning nonetheless. If a corporation is a personal services corporation, then it must pay a 35% tax rate on all income. This generally includes service businesses such as doctors, accountants, lawyers, engineers, architects, and consultants. But if your main business is selling products, then this rule will not affect you.

Those people who should use a corporate form of business entity are people who have some concerns about liability exposure, and who fit the following categories:

- They have a business with a large amount of inventory, and need to accumulate capital for this purpose.
- They have a need to increase their capital for future marketing expansion programs.
- They are thinking of going public at some point in the future.
- They need to take advantage of some fringe benefits such as health care insurance.

The main reason for forming a corporation is to be protected from liability or to later request a public offering. But if neither of these reasons fit your business profile, then don't bother to form a corporation. It is also true, that many individuals who form corporations do not keep up with the proper paperwork filings. If you are the type of person who is bored by such formalities, then don't form a corporation. Form a limited liability company instead.

5. THE "S" CORPORATION

Corporations that elect an "S" status, are not subject to double taxation. In fact," S" corporations don't pay taxes. Instead, the profits are transferred to the owner's personal tax return where they are merged with other income that adjusts total income from all sources to determine the IRS tax bracket. To be an "S" corporation you must file form 2553 with the IRS within the first 75 days of the tax year to qualify for "S" benefits in that tax year.

ADVANTAGES OF "S" CORPORATIONS:

Besides avoiding double taxation, you can also eliminate up to 50% of your Social Security and Medicare taxes. The key is in understanding that you pay self-employment taxes on wages, salaries, and bonuses. You do not pay tax on dividends earned! Your share on undistributed earnings is classified as dividends and not wages, and therefore is treated as any actual dividend distribution. Dividends and undistributed earnings are not subject to self-employment tax. Therefore, the key is to pay yourself as small a salary as possible, and as much in dividends as possible. In this way you can eliminate most of your Social Security tax. For example, let's say that Dave Brown earned $90,000.00 from his "S" corporation. If he pays himself this amount in salary, then it is all subject to a 15.3% self-employment tax, which would be $13,770.00. If, however, Dave pays himself a reasonable salary of $40,000.00, and takes the other $50,000.00 as dividends he would save $7,650.00 for every year that he does this. If properly invested, it would amount to a tidy sum to add to his Social Security check after he retires. The key is to pay yourself a reasonable salary, otherwise the I.R.S. may conclude that it is actually wages earned, and you would end up paying back the taxes owed. Most advisors think that a $40,000.00 - $50,000.00 per year pay-check is a reasonable salary, but check with your tax advisor before exercising this benefit.

Income Splitting

Our regressive tax tables elevate us into higher tax brackets the more money we make. To avoid this, it is a good idea to split the profits among family members rather than you as the owner declaring 100% of your salary for tax calculations. By splitting your salary among your spouse and children, you lower the tax bracket for all concerned, and thus pay far less taxes. An "S" corporation can allow you this same benefit. For example, let us suppose that Ben and Lois Johnson manage a Sole Proprietorship, which earned $112,850.00 last year, and caused them to pay $24,265.00 in federal taxes alone. By setting up an "S" corporation and providing their three children with 15% of the stock each, then each child would be taxed on 15% of the gain, and the parents would be taxed on 55% of the gain. Each child would then pay $2,239.00 in taxes, and the parents would pay $10,554.00. The savings to the family would be $6,994.00, which is considerable. Here is how the numbers play out:

Tax payable by parents as a sole proprietorship	$ 24,265.00
Tax payable by all three children	$ 6,717.00
Tax payable by parents using split income technique	$ 10,554/00
Total taxes paid by the family	$ 17,271.00
Net savings to the family using the split income technique	$ 6,994.00

"S" Corporation Losses

Unlike a regular corporation, an "S" corporation owner can pass through any losses onto his personal tax return, and then use the losses to offset any earned income from other sources. This is another great benefit.

DISADVANTAGES OF "S" CORPORATIONS:

- All stock must be owned by American citizens or a U.S. resident.
- You must have fewer than 100 stockholders.
- It must be a domestic corporation formed in America.
- You can only have one class of stock.
- Only individuals and certain types of limited trusts can be stockholders.
- You cannot accumulate capital at lower corporate rates as with a regular corporation.
- All profits, whether you take them out or not, are taxable in the year earned.

Who should form an "S" corporation? Typically, people who made less than $118,500.00 in 2015.

6. LIMITED LIABILIITY COMPANIES (LLCs)

Question. What state was the first to introduce Limited Liability Companies (LLCs)? Clue – they have more cattle than people. Answer: Wyoming, of all places, in 1977. Now LLCs are accepted by all 50 states. An LLC is essentially a hybrid cross between a limited partnership and a corporation. If there is only one owner, it is classified as a Sole Proprietor as far as the IRS is concerned, because all you have to do is file a Schedule C with your federal tax return. If there is more than one owner, you file a partnership form 1065. Regardless of how you file, the LLC will protect you from liability the same as a corporation.

ADVANTAGES OF AN LLC:

None of the Restrictions of an "S" Corporation

You can have any number of investors, including foreign investors. This creates a lot of flexibility compared to the "S" corporation.

Business Loss Treatment

Due to the fact that the IRS treats LLCs similar to Sole Proprietorships and partnerships, any losses are trans-ferred to the owner's personal tax return.

Asset Protection

If you form an LLC, it is wise to place a clause in your forming documents that states that no new members of the LLC are allowed without the approval of the other members. This prevents creditors from becoming mem-bers. Therefore, if you lose a law-suit, a creditor cannot get the stock or become an unwanted partner. The only way a creditor can proceed is through a charging order, which provides that any distribution that goes to an LLC member will, in fact, go to the creditor. This is a nega-tive for the creditor, because if the LLC has undistributed income, the creditor would be taxed on the member's share of the undistributed income, just as the debtor-member would. This is the case even though the creditor did not receive the distribution! Most creditors would hesitate before putting themselves in such a position.

DISADVANTAGES OF A LIMITED LIABILITY COMPANY

Unlike "S" corporations that can save on Social Security and Medicare taxes by distributing dividends along with salaries, that is not the case with LLCs. As I mentioned earlier, an LLC is taxed like a Sole Proprietorship, and therefore all earnings are taxed. There are some special circumstances where this does not apply, which I suggest you discuss with your tax advisor.

SUMMARY

It is obvious by the points mentioned in this chapter, and the previous one, of the importance placed in choosing a business entity carefully, so that it meets the specific requirements of your goals and objectives. I have provided you with an overview of business entities in order to educate you on some of the issues involved. In this way, you should be able to grasp a good, basic understanding of this subject, and ask the right questions as you move forward. Realize, of course, that this chapter was not meant to be exhaustive on this subject, and you would be well advised to work with your tax advisor and a good business lawyer before forming your business entity.

The attention I have devoted in these last two chapters to owning your own business, should be of no surprise to you when I tell you I am a staunch small business advocate. I arrived at this way of thinking due to many years of seeing men and women of limited education, and simple means, go on to succeed beyond their wildest imaginations. Today, these same people have already retired, or are well on their way towards enjoying a terrific retirement that they richly deserve. Instead of working for someone else and allowing them to keep all the profits, they took matters into their own hands, and with the help of the Lord created their own destiny. You can do the same. All it takes is time, effort, and dedication to your own success. By effectively using the tax benefits of business ownership, and building a good solid business enterprise, you can definitely fast-track your way towards a very prosperous future assuming you have God as your silent partner.

I should also state, that in all fairness to some readers, the last two chapters perhaps made you feel a little overwhelmed with the knowledge I have provided about owning your own business. Realize, however, that you gained enough knowledge equivalent to a university degree in business, and at a fraction of the cost. You should now find yourself far more qualified to start and manage your own business, or help some other family member or friend to do likewise. You are now at a great advantage, which I don't want you to discount. Knowledge is power, and if you do decide to own your own business, a careful study of these chapters should provide you with the self-confidence to dig deeper to explore the possibilities, which are endless.

By checking in with God every day, you will have the very best business partner that any man or woman could ask for, because He has said so many times in the Bible that He does not want to see people mired down in debt, but to be free and to prosper. So why not take Him up on His offer, and strive towards financial security for you and your loved ones? Tennessee Williams said it best when he commented, "You can be young without money, but you can't be old without it!" At least not in America!

SECTION FOUR

INVESTING AND SPENDING WISELY

Know what you own, and know why you own it!
– Peter Lynch

How many millionaires became wealthy
investing in saving accounts?
– Robert Allen

CHAPTER ELEVEN

SMART WAYS TO PURCHASE BIG TICKET ITEMS

An investment in knowledge, pays the best interest!
– Benjamin Franklin

IN THIS AND the next chapter we will cover methods for purchasing automobiles and real estate, which can often be the biggest spending decisions most household have to make. Such decisions can have devastating consequences if we make a mistake due to a lack of knowledge. On the other hand, the right decision can result in many thousands of dollars in your favor, which can be used to reduce debt or invest for retirement. Other household buying decisions are often dwarfed by these two large budget expense items. So let's take a look at automobiles first.

PURCHASING AN AUTOMOBILE

It is clear by the figures that Americans are in love with their automobiles, because there are more than 250 million on the roads, with an average age of 11.4 years based on the latest reports.

In 2015 more than 16 million new cars were sold including everything from sedans, crossovers, hatchbacks, luxury, SUVs, convertibles, coupes, minivans, wagons, trucks, and cars driven with diesel fuel, electric, or hybrids. There are more than 60 models to choose from in all. Some pundits make the case that the automobile is indispensable to the American household due to the huge size of our country, and the distances we travel to get to work. Public transportation is not always available, and commuting by motorcycle or bicycle is not everyone's cup of tea. Car Pooling, and the use of HOV lanes on the highways have helped some, but in reality personal ownership of an automobile is the most popular choice. So, we have a lot of decisions to make if we want to negotiate the best deal for ourselves, because personal transportation is expensive. Do I buy new or used? Should I pay cash or get financing? What about trading my current car? What about depreciation, fuel consumption, safety, and maintenance issues? How do I avoid being scammed? You need to be prepared, because if you are not, you will be taken advantage of, and it could cost you plenty. So let's explore our options:

NEW CAR PURCHASES:

Unless you are completely out of debt with plenty of money to spare, I generally recommend that you refrain from purchasing new vehicles due to their rapid devaluation based on prescribed depreciation schedules. I like to invest in assets that have the potential to appreciate in the future, rather than an investment that has a built-in guarantee of dropping in value. However, I also understand that a family man is driving precious cargo when his kids are in the back seat, and therefore the latest safety features are often considered. I get it. Also, certain types of occupations might require a late model vehicle to demonstrate being successful when working with rich clients.

It is important to remember that an automobile is a product like anything else you purchase, except that it often comes with a much higher price ticket. Therefore, to ensure you get the best value for your money, you need to do your research, and ask lots of questions. Hopefully, by the time you have read this chapter, you will know what questions to ask, what resources are available to you, and a check-list that is easy to follow in assisting you to make the very best decision for you and your family.

You will find the same vehicle with the same price structure at every dealership you visit. So, the only leverage you have is if there is more than one dealer competing for your business. Once you walk onto a dealership lot, however, you have just thrown away any leverage you had. Today, thanks to the Internet, you can do most of your car shopping from the convenience of your laptop computer. You can gain a tremendous amount of information from reputable websites such as:

www.kellybluebook.com www.edmunds.com
www.consumerreports.com www.carclearancedeals.com
www.truecar.com www.cars.com www.cargurus.com

Also, for the small amount of $39.95 you can obtain a great buying report for the final car of your choice by contacting: www.fightingchance.com

So with these thoughts in mind, let's take a look at some steps you can take to avoid blunders and errors in purchasing the best new car for you at a price that does not cause you to leave money on the table. You may be thinking that this is too much work. However, it is a well known fact that many people spend more time planning their next vacation than they do spending a few hours purchasing a new car that could cost them $30,000.00 or more, and which they may be driving for many, many years to come. So spending the time to buy a car wisely can sometimes save you enough money to pay for that well earned vacation twice over!

A PROVEN SYSTEM TO GET THE BEST PRICE ON A NEW CAR PURCHASE

If you complete these steps you will save thousands of dollars!

Step One: The first items to consider are your transportation needs, not just now, but also in the future. Functionality is important. For instance, how many passengers do you need to carry? What type of driving do you mainly do – highway, streets, off-road, ice and snow? Do you drive far to work, and therefore is fuel efficiency a consideration? What safety features are important to you? Do you have a need for all-wheel drive, or towing needs? Is cargo capacity sufficient? Will it fit comfortably in your garage? How about children's car seat fittings?

Step Two: If you are not a cash customer, then your budget must be considered, and I recommend that your monthly payments not exceed 15% of your net take home pay. If, for instance, your monthly net income is $3,000.00, then keep your new car payment at about $450.00. Before going above that figure you may want to consider increasing your down payment to keep your payments in line, or paying-off another debt. Do not fall for the dealer trick where they reduce the monthly payment to suit your budget by increasing the number of months to pay for the car. Dealers have the option to increase a 48 month loan to 52 months or longer. 60 month loans can be stretched to 65 months etc. The longer it takes to pay off the car, the more it costs you in interest charges.

Step Three: The next step is to create a folder that should contain the following information:

a. You need a copy of your latest credit report and FICO score. If you don't have your score, you put yourself at a disadvantage with a dealer who may charge a higher interest rate based on a lower score than what you actually have.

b. Assemble new car quotes from reputable websites mentioned above.

c. Be sure to have a copy of your Guaranteed Savings certificate from Truecar.com

d. Get your car loan approval in advance. For fast service you can go to: www.lightstream.com. If your FICO score is low, try: www.autocreditexpress.com. Put at least 20% down to ensure you are not upside down later when you trade-in. Never extend your loan beyond 48 months, and ensure all your current credit balances are below 50% of your credit limits to avoid having your FICO score dropped. The sweet spot is having a FICO score above 680 to qualify for prime rates. Below 680 is considered sub-prime with higher interest rates. If your score is below 550 it is best to forget financing due to a much higher rate being charged. Clean up your credit first, and then apply. Later, when working with a dealer, you should compare your loan figures against what dealer financing might be able to do.

e. If you are contemplating a number of vehicles, you may wish to use your laptop to get free spreadsheets from www.carbuyingtips.com.

f. Get an insurance quote for the car you are thinking of purchasing.

g. Obtain your real trade-in market value. Remember, dealers never give you fair market value. They generally offer a wholesale price, which could be $1,000 to $5,000 less than fair market value. So treat your trade-in as a separate deal, and try to sell it yourself, or use EBay Motors. Also, why you are at it, obtain some extended warranty quotes.

Step Four: Now you are ready to test drive the car of your choice. During the test, speak as little as possible, because everything you say, just like being in court, will be used against you. If the salesperson feels you are a payment buyer, he will condition the conversation accordingly by finding out what payment you can comfortably afford. Be quick to let him know that you only deal with the total price because you have pre- approved financing. Always inspect the car during the day to highlight the color scheme, and possible dents or other defects. While driving, keep the radio off to hear the hum of the engine and how quiet it is. Try accelerating to determine how quickly the car speeds up. Use the air-conditioning and heating system, and be sure to sit in the back to feel what it is like for your passengers.

Keep in mind that your goal is never to purchase on the first visit to the dealer. Your main task is to obtain pricing and options from the MSRP sticker on the car. Truecar. com can provide you with prices of what other buyers in your area have paid for the car you are interested in buying, as well as MSRP and invoice price. Use your smart phone to take a picture of the MSRP sticker information. You should also ask the salesman for a copy of the dealers factory invoice to determine what the dealer actually paid. Many dealers will provide this information, but if they don't, then obtain it from one of the websites mentioned above.

With a copy of the factory invoice, you can offer a dealer somewhere between 3% to 4% above dealer cost, and it will probably be accepted. Many dealers get by with a 3% profit margin as you will soon find out. The factory invoice price lists all option packages, floor mats, trims, and destination charges. There will generally be a hold back, which is about 3% minus destination and delivery charges. The Holdback is given to the dealer after he sells the car. Do not make the mistake of comparing the MSRP price with the invoice price, and make sure the invoice the salesman is providing you compares with your own research. One of the best places to get a dealer factory invoice for the car you are buying is to go to: www. fightingchance.com. Other sites offer this information for free, but it may not be as updated. Here is a simple example of how the numbers work:

Factory invoice price paid by the dealer	$25,500.00
Minus the Holdback	
(paid to dealer when the car is sold)	$ 765.00 (3%)
MSRP price	$27,900.00
Destination charge	$ 495.00
Factory dealer incentive	$ 400.00
Customer rebate	$ 500.00

In this example, the actual dealer cost is $25,500.00 - $400.00 incentive – Holdback $765.00 = $24,335.00. With this information you can now offer a price of $25,065.00 ($24,335.00 plus $730.00 (3%). Knowing the true dealer cost provides you with a lot of power in negotiations. Isn't the world-wide web a wonderful thing?

Step Five: Take pause to consider the long term cost of ownership. Some vehicles depreciate faster than others, to say nothing of differences in maintenance, fuel and insurance costs. You should also ask if sales for the car you want are up or down, and does the average dealer sell a lot or a few of your particular model. Are current inventories high or low? Answers to these questions provide you with a little more power in negotiating the final price.

Step Six: You are now getting closer to closing the deal. You have successfully leveled the playing field, and positioned yourself well regarding final negotiations. You have completed your new car folder, which contains your latest credit report and FICO score; you have received pre-loan approval; you have obtained an insurance quote to eliminate surprises later, and you have a copy of the factory invoice along with a copy of the MSRP information.

A Quick Word on Negotiating: When negotiating, it is always helpful to fully understand what the rules of the game are, and what your opponent is trying to achieve. For instance, you want to get the best price on your trade-in, the lowest purchase price on your new car, the lowest interest rate on your new loan, no add-ons, and as little extra fees as possible. The dealer on the other hand, wants to get the lowest price he can on your trade-in, and the highest price for the car he is selling you. The dealer also wants to do the financing so he can get the highest rate, credit and gap insurance, plenty of add- ons, and add plenty of fees. Now that we know what both parties want, it becomes clearer in the way you negotiate your best deal.

During negotiations, try to keep the following points in mind:

a. Take someone along to avoid intimidation tactics when they try to gang up on you.

b. Be sure to remember the date the car was shipped. You can find it on the top left hand side of the MSRP invoice. This will give you some idea of how long the dealer has kept the car on the lot. Dealers pay bank flooring costs to fund their inventories. The longer the car stays on the lot, the more it costs the dealer, so they want to sell their oldest cars first to avoid further interest costs. If you experience tough negotiations, and you still want the car, then ask for the same model that just arrived on the lot recently. This is a good ploy to use to get what you really want – the very best price!

c. When the salesman leaves the room, it is not a good idea to talk too much. Why? The phone intercom is sometimes deliberately left on so they can hear the conversation.

d. When the dealer says if he can't beat all competition he will give you $500.00, don't believe it. It is very difficult to obtain paperwork from another dealer to show proof.

e. The best time of year to buy should also be considered. Generally, late December when car lots are empty of customers who are Christmas shopping, is one good time. Another good time is between July and October when dealers are trying to clear out old stock to make room for the new models.

Step Seven: Now it is time to close the deal. You have selected your dream car, with any options you desire. You have test driven the car to your satisfaction, and, thanks to all your pre-planning, you used your new car folder with your FICO score, pre-loan approval, and review of dealer invoice costs to work your very best deal. You also have your insurance in place. Carefully review the contract before signing. Study all the figures and make sure the dealer is not adding extra fees to make up for what he lost on the sales price. Tip: many car buyers are worn out by the time they get to the F&I department (finance and insurance), and are quick to sign to get the whole matter over with. Keep this in mind.

Now you have a full tank of gas, and you are on your way! As I mentioned earlier, it may seem like a lot of work, but if you consider the money you have saved, which often runs into the thousands of dollars, it is well worth it. For instance, if you spent say 10 hours from start to finish, and it resulted in you saving $4,000.00, it works out to $400.00 per hour! Do you make that kind of money where you work? Enough said. Case closed.

PURCHASING A USED CAR:

If you make the decision to buy a used car, you are already thousands of dollars ahead of the game, due to the fact that you have already successfully passed the rapid car depreciation on to the original owner. The best used cars are those two to three years of age, with no more than 12,000 miles per year on the clock. Also, cars more than five-years old are generally not financeable by banks. Many of the points made in purchasing a new car also apply to buying a used car, with some additional steps you need to take to minimize risk, and get the best deal. So, let's take a look at purchasing from a private party first.

Buying From a Private Party

The sources for used cars are endless, and include used car dealers, rental car companies, auctions, and private parties. You can check a number of websites to get the information you are looking for, and limit your search to two or three choices. You can check out the following auto websites: www.autobytel.com, www.carpoint.com, www.carsdirect.com, www.cars.com, www.usedcars.com, www.edmunds.com, www.truecar.com, www.autotrader. com, and www.craigslist.com, to name a few.

Use your phone effectively by calling the sellers and asking them certain questions before a visit (see also the Used Car Checklists mentioned below). Some of the questions can be asked when you are test driving the car.

The Process

Before physically test driving the car, I am assuming you have already checked pricing from sources such as Kelly Blue Book, or Edmunds.com, and that you have worked your budget, arranged for bank pre-approval, and developed an understanding with your insurance agent to get a quick insurance binder when you purchase. In test driving the vehicle be sure to have your driving license and insurance card with you. You need to see the auto title to ensure it is free and clear of liens. Also, verify ownership by checking the seller's driving license. While in the seller's drive-way, check to see if there are oil stains. If so, ask why. If all goes well, your next stop is to have your mechanic check the car out. This may cost you $50 - $100. Don't be passive when working with your mechanic. Get involved to ensure that all safety features are checked: exterior, interior, tires, engine, frame, automatic transmission, steering, suspension and miscellaneous items. Two great websites you can check, that will provide comprehensive used car check-lists, includes: www.dmv. org, and www.popularmechanics.com.

You also need to check the vehicle history by going to either: www.carfax.com, or www.autocheck.com. All you need is the 17 digit VIN number. Also, if there is a lien on the car, then you need to work directly with the bank to pay off the balance and get your name substituted on the title. If you pay cash, then arrange to meet with the seller at your bank to obtain a cashier's check in exchange for the seller signing off the title. Be sure, prior to closing the deal, to obtain all car maintenance records, owner's manual, and all keys, including wheel lock keys, otherwise you will not be able to change the tires!

Negotiating with a Dealer

Many dealers sell their cars as "certified used cars." Do not allow the word "certified" to distract you from doing your normal due diligence. Federal law does require the buyer to be given a "Buyer's Guide," on all used cars sold by dealers. The purpose is to tell the buyer whether the car is being sold "As-Is," or whether there is a remaining factory warranty. It also tells the buyer what obligations the dealer has committed to. Many complaints happen because a salesperson says the car has a warranty, when in actual fact the sticker says the car is being sold "As-Is," which means you have no protection. Remember, the sticker takes precedence over what that salesperson said. So if the Buyer's Guide is not posted on the window, leave the lot. Dealers generally pay $3,000 - $4,000 less than market value for a used car, so they have plenty of room to negotiate a lower price. Most pricing sites have three categories of a car's condition – bad, fair or good, and each has a different price value attached. Keep in mind that if you are using the Kelly Blue Book for pricing, the dealer will probably say he uses NADA values, which are higher because they add for dealer re-conditioning costs.

In this chapter, I have provided you with a lot of detail for the sole purpose of helping you get the very best deal on an automobile purchase with the hope that your savings, along with other savings from your tax planning, budgeting, and expense cost control system, will assist you in paying off your debt, or invest for your future. Even though we are negotiating for the best price possible, let us not forget that we are doing it to be good stewards of God's assets. When we work in this humanistic secular world, we always have to remember the admonition that Jesus made in Matthew 10:16, when He said, "I am sending you out like sheep among wolves. Therefore be as shrewd as snakes and as innocent as doves." With this thought in mind, you need to pray about what you wish to accomplish; do your homework; attempt to become as knowledgeable as possible; be honest in all your dealings, and finally, by putting on the armor of Christ, you will be very pleased with the ultimate outcome.

CHAPTER TWELVE

ARE YOU READY FOR REAL ESTATE?

Real Estate cannot be lost or stolen, nor can it be carried away. Purchased with common sense, paid in full, and managed with reasonable care, it is about the safest investment in the world!

– President Franklin Roosevelt

SINCE THE REAL ESTATE and stock market crash in 2008, we have seen in some states like Arizona, Nevada, and Florida, home prices plunge as much as 50%. An analysis by www.Zillow.com states that some markets, like New York and Los Angeles are now higher than pre-2008, while cities like Chicago are still well below previous values. What is interesting to note, however, is that rents did not drop 50% at the time of the 2008 real estate crash! In fact, they remained about the same, which at the same time demonstrated to investors that they could double their cash-on-cash return at those lower prices.

Zillow.com claims the average home value in the U.S. at the end of 2016 was $201,900.00 for a total value for all homes of $29 trillion. Meanwhile, the federal reserve states there is just under $8 trillion in outstanding mortgages. Obviously, home equity represents a considerable amount of wealth for American families.

There are approximately 130 million homes in the U.S., which are roughly divided between home owners (2/3), and renters (1/3). Home owner vacancies, according to www.census. gov/housing, are about 1.8%, while rental vacancies are 6.9%. It is also of interest to note that Millennials, a.k.a. generation Y (born 1980 to early 2000s), represents 37% of all renters, indicating either a reluctance to purchase based on an uncertain future, or they don't have the savings built up enough to make the decision. Others like the idea of renting, especially if they think they will be moving later for career advancement.

RENTING VS. BUYING A HOME

Robert Shiller, who won the Nobel prize in economic science in 2013, states that home prices have only risen 0.375 percent annually over the last 126 years, when adjusting for inflation, and he goes on to make the case that people might be better off renting. He stated: "Disregarding the special amenities that many people value in home ownership, it would be hugely better invested in the stock market." So, who am I to argue with a great man like Robert Shiller? Unfortunately, I must, because the facts prove otherwise, which we will soon discover. Before leaving this point, however, I should also mention that the value of a dollar today, is worth about 5% when compared with just over 100 years ago, when the Federal Reserve System was created. So, even though Shiller is correct in pointing out a 0.375% annual increase for home values overall, after adjusting for inflation, he must admit that home ownership has been a good hedge against inflation, and will continue to do so for the future. Unfortunately, renters suffer from inflation as rents are increased and provide nothing in the form of future wealth.

So, the decision to rent or buy boils down to several factors. If a family can rent a home for less than the cost of purchasing, and if they put the difference into the stock market, it is possible to sometimes come out ahead. However, there are a number of variables that must be considered, such as how the stock market returns do, how long the family stays in the home, and how sharp are they in buying at a good price, and arranging good financing. In general, though, the truth comes out by using an illustration.

If you purchase a home for $250,000.00, financed for 30 years, with a fixed rate of 4%, and a down payment of 20% to avoid PMI insurance costs, the monthly principal and interest would be $955.00 per month. Add to this cost the annual property tax ($2,000.00/12 = $167.00 per month), and the annual property insurance ($400.00/12 = $33.00/month), and we have a month outlay of $1,155.00, principal, interest, taxes and insurance (PITI). To rent this same home, let us assume a rent of $1,300.00 per month. Now we look three-years down the road and look at the new numbers:

All numbers rounded:

Renting the Home:

Security Deposit	$ 1,300.00		
36 rent payments	$46,800.00		
Total rent paid after three-years	$48,100.00		

	Example 1	Example 2	
Buying the home:	20% Down	10% Down	Renting
Down payment -	$ 50,000.00	$25,000.00	
Closing costs – 1%	$ 2,500.00	$ 2,500.00	
Maintenance costs – 1%	$ 7,500.00	$ 7,500.00	
PMI Insurance cost – 1%	$ -0-	$ 7,500.00	
Three-year payments -	$ 41,580.00	$45,864.00	
Total Cost after three-years	$ 101,580.00	$88,364.00	$48,100.00

In Example 1 the down payment of $50,000.00 is a form of savings for the buyer, which created $50,000.00 equity in the home. The home is worth $250,000.00, but the buyer now only owes $200,000.00 against it (in reality, the mortgage balance is less due to principle reduction over the last three-years). So we subtract, for simplicity, the $50,000.00 down-payment. Now the difference between renting and buying is only $3,480.00 in favor of renting, assuming the rent has not been increased during the three-year period, which is unlikely. Let us assume the buyer is in a low tax bracket rate of 15% (that would be annual earnings of less than $75,300.00 for a couple filing jointly in 2016). They are able to take advantage of a tax write-off for property tax ($2,000.00 x 3 years = $6,000.00), property insurance ($400.00 x 3 years = $1,200.00), and interest paid on the mortgage of $23,571.00 for three-years. These figures total $30,771.00 x .15 = a tax savings over three-years of $4,616.00.

The above numbers make the case that if someone is expecting to rent for a short while, then it is probably the best decision for them. However, renting for three-years or more puts the numbers in favor of buying, and it should get better for the buyer going forward due to principal reduction on the mortgage, which was well over $11,000.00 after three-years, plus the possibility of appreciation. The renter generates no equity build-up, and if he decides to purchase in the future, it will probably be at a higher price. Even if the home does not increase in value, it would still provide a $250,000.00 nest egg to add to the buyer's retirement portfolio after the last payment is made, creating a forced saving plan. The renter may still be renting into retirement! This might help explain why, according to a Forbes Magazine article (10.15.2015), a federal reserve study showed that the average renter's net worth was $5,400.00 in 2013, whereas the average home owner net worth was $195,400! Allowing for a 3% annual increase, it was estimated that the 2016 figures would be $225,000.00 for homeowners, and about $5,400.00 for renters. That is higher than a multiple of 40 in favor of homeowners on a lifetime financial achievement scale.

For a family that makes a 10% down payment instead of 20%, I demonstrate in Example 2 how the figures would run. Obviously with less than 20% down, the buyer would have to pay PMI insurance, which generally runs around 1% annually of the purchase price, depending on your credit score. The PMI can be removed once the buyer has 20% equity in the property, but it must be applied for. The figures show that it would take a little longer than three-years for a buyer to come out ahead. Here again, I have not taken into consideration any annual rent increases during the first three-years for a renter, nor have

I credited the buyer with principal reduction on the mortgage, which is in excess of $11,000.00, to say nothing of possible appreciation of the property.

It should also be pointed out that substantial savings can be gained by entering into a 15 year mortgage rather than 30 years. Take a look at the difference in the numbers:

$200,000.00 payable over 30 years at 4% annual interest rate:
Total interest paid would amount to $143,739.00
Actual monthly payment would be $ 955.00
Total payments made would equal $343,739.00

$200,000.00 payable over 15 years at 3.50% (a lower annual interest rate)
Total interest paid would amount to $ 57,400.00
Actual monthly payment would be $ 1,430.00
Total payments made would equal $257,400.00

Your Big Savings Pay-Off

This is where the "rubber meets the road," because by simply increasing your monthly payment by $475.00, ($1430.00 - $955.00), you would pay-off the mortgage in half the time, and save yourself $86,451.00 in payments and interest! Do you have ways in your budget to reduce expenses by $475.00, or increase your monthly income by that amount? This is where getting completely out of debt, and adhering to your 12% savings plan, really pays off. By following the double down debt reduction program mentioned in chapter 7, you can now clearly see how much easier it is to come up with the extra $475.00, but not if you are still in debt, or not abiding by the budget system we discussed in Chapter Five.

If you absolutely must take out a 30 year mortgage, then I suggest you pay one or two extra payments each year, perhaps out of your tax refund. These extra payments will help you to pay-off the loan faster because your second payment goes 100% to principle loan balance reduction. Those extra payments provide you with the best return on your money than any other asset. You will literally save thousands of dollars over the life of the loan, and own your home free and clear much faster.

So far we have looked at purchasing a home, versus renting it, purely through the lens of numbers. However, there is far more to say about this subject. Home ownership means that you actually own the place. This fact provides emotional and psychological satisfaction in knowing that you have real stability in your home life. Nobody can make you move, and if you have a fixed rate of interest on your loan, it will never go up. This means that your mortgage payment, excluding property taxes and insurance, when expressed as a percentage of monthly income, will, in all likelihood, go down in the future, making it less costly. Renters, on the other hand, are subject to rent increases, and can often be forced to move on a thirty-day written notice from the landlord.

So, I am firmly convinced that buying a home pays off in the long term. I favor home ownership not only for a good defense to protect against inflation, but also for the financial leverage it provides. For instance, if you invested $1,000.00 and it increased 5% in the first year, you would have leveraged $50.00 on your investment. On the other hand, if you invested $250,000.00 and gained a return of 5%, you would gain a $12,500.00 leveraged return on your investment. Now you may not have $250,000.00, but by purchasing a home worth $250,000.00 and taking out a $200,000.00 mortgage, you get the benefit of the 5% inflation that increases the $250,000.00 home value to $262,500.00, which you get the benefit of, and not the mortgage lender who loaned you the money. This is the beauty of working with large numbers as they tend to amplify your gains, and create a fast track to wealth accumulation.

Depending upon your circumstances, you will no doubt act according to your own best interests. However, if you have paid off your debt, and saved a sufficient down payment to acquire a home, then I want to delve further with you into ways and means of you owning either your first home, or whether you intend to purchase a second or third home.

DETERMING WHAT HOME VALUE YOU CAN AFFORD BASED ON INCOME

The table below shows you a quick rule of thumb to show you the maximum home value you can afford to purchase based on your annual gross income. For instance, if you earn $60,000.00 gross annual income, you would then multiply it by 4.6, provided you lock-in a 4% fixed interest rate on a 30 year mortgage. This would qualify you for a home priced of about $276,000.00. At a 5% interest rate, you would qualify for a home worth about $252,000.00. Can you now see how a good FICO score can work in your favor by qualifying you for a lower interest rate?

THE MAXIMUM YOU CAN BORROW BASED ON YOUR GROSS ANNUAL INCOME	
Mortgage Rates	Multiply Your Gross Income by the below Figure
3%	5.0
4%	4.6
5%	4.2
6%	3.8
8%	3.2

Note: If you are self-employed, then use your net profit (income) before taxes as your qualifying figure

Table 12:1

FINDING THE ELUSIVE DOWN PAYMENT REQUIREMENT

Buying a home is a long-term project and requires thought and planning to make it happen for many struggling young families. First, it is a myth to believe that a 20% down payment is required to purchase a home. It is not true, which I will soon demonstrate. Also, 87% of first-time home buyers think they need at least 10% down payment to qualify according to the National Association of Realtors. This is also not true. According to national statistics, the average down payment is about 6%, and there are loan programs where a buyer can purchase a home with zero down payment. Here are some options:

1. **Federal Housing Authority (FHA) Loans:** These loans can be obtained with a 3.5% down payment, and 100% of the down payment can be given by a relative. FHA mortgage insurance premium (MIP), and fees require 1.75% of the loan amount upfront, and 0.85% is payable each year on the current loan balance. On a $200,000.00 loan, for instance, it would require $3,500.00 upfront, and about $141.00 payment each month. The upfront fee, however, can be rolled into the loan amount and therefore does not need to be paid in cash. FICO scores can be as low as 580 to qualify. About 40% of home buyers under the age of 40, use FHA financing, but older buyers are using this program as well.

2. **Veteran Affairs (VA) Loans:** Current and former military personnel qualify for this loan program with zero down payment. VA mortgage insurance and fees require a 2.15% upfront fee for first-time home buyers who make less than a 5% down payment. The fee can be rolled into the loan amount. No monthly mortgage insurance is required, and FICO scores can be accepted as low as 650 and above.

3. **US Department of Agriculture (USDA) Loans:** Also known as Rural Development Housing loans, they are 100% financeable, for non-urban areas. About 97% of U.S. land mass is eligible including suburban neighborhoods across the country. Buyers must make 115% or less of their area's median income. Mortgage insurance fees are 1% of the loan amount upfront and 0.35% payment per year based on the current loan amount balance. For example, a loan of $200,000.00 would require $2,000.00 upfront, which can be rolled into the loan, and then they pay $58.00 per month. FICO scores must be above 640.

4. **Conventional 97 Loans:** Fannie Mae (Federal National Mortgage Association), offers these loans with a 3% down payment, and 100% of the down payment can come from a financial gift. Conventional loans do not come with an upfront fee like FHA, VA or USDA loans. However, PMI insurance is required for any down payment lower than 20% based on credit score, and the rate can range between 0.75% - 1.5% of the loan amount per year. You will need good credit to qualify for this program, which suits borrowers with good credit, who have 3% down payment, and additional money for closing costs. FHA is probably more cost effective than this program.

5. **Home Ready Mortgages, and Home Possible Advantage Loans:** These loans are offered by Fannie Mae with 3% down payments. There is also a Home Path Closing Costs Assistance Program

6. **Down Payment Assistant Programs:** This program is designed to help eligible buyers bridge the gap between their savings and the down payment requirement. Check out the U.S. Housing and Urban Development website for more information at: www.hud.gov.

7. **Other Creative Method:** If you are fed up of renting, but don't have all the money to qualify for a home purchase, try finding a partner. It could be a relative or friend that is willing to buy a property with you. Be sure to enter into a legal binding contract that spells out how you solve an issue of one partner later wanting out, or a case of disability, death, or divorce. You might also consider purchasing a cheaper property that requires less out-of-pocket expense that you can leverage later into a larger home when equity increases.

For the ambitious person who wants to purchase his or her own home, there are many ways to make it happen. All you need is the will. Assuming for the moment that you have already implemented a good family budget plan, used the double-down method to get out of debt, cleaned up any loose-ends on your credit report, determined your new FICO score, and are applying the principle of a dollar saved is a dollar earned as mentioned in Table 6:1, you are well on your way to home ownership.

INCENTIVES FOR OWNING REAL PROPERTY

In America, unlike many other parts of the world, our government and business leaders encourage home ownership, and provide many forms of financing to help American families to achieve their goals. This explains why the U.S. has the highest home ownership in the world.

Owning your own property has four practical benefits: 1) it will force you to save for your retirement, whereas renting doesn't: 2) if you pay-off the mortgage before you retire, your social security check will stretch a lot further: 3) owning property is a great hedge against the ravages of inflation, which eats into the purchasing power of your money every year. However, as a property owner, you enjoy the benefit of an increase in value due to inflation. In other words, you benefit from inflation rather than suffer its consequences: 4) owning property is a great tax free investment, because it grows in value without you having to pay taxes on the gains. As of this writing, if you are a married couple selling your property, the first $500,000.00 in gain is tax free, and $250,000.00 for a single person. These are great tax shelter terms.

THE HUNT BEGINS:

We all want similar things when it comes to purchasing a property for our family. We want the lowest price, in the best neighborhood, with the most favorable financing terms. We also want the right floor plan, amenities, garage, and lot size. We need the property to be located in a good school district for the kids, a low crime area, and most importantly, we want to buy at the best time for future appreciation of the property. At some point, however, we will find ourselves compromising our perfect dream home to fit the realities of our circumstances. We need to figure out our purchase budget, with payments not to exceed 25% of our net monthly take home income, if possible.

Do you now have the requisite 20% down payment to eliminate PMI insurance, and obtain the lowest interest rate, because your FICO score is now above 700? Or, will you be taking advantage of one of the low down payment plans mentioned earlier? Are you completely out of debt, or are all outstanding debts less than 50% of the credit limit for each obligation? Can you live with two-bedrooms rather than three, or a two-story rather than a ranch style? Once these questions have been answered, you should pull your own credit report to ensure it is clean, and to re-check your FICO score. Contact your lender and obtain a pre-qualification letter so you know in advance just how much of a mortgage you qualify for. Aided with this information, you can now approach real estate agents in your chosen market area for assistance in finding a property, and they will clamor for your business.

Working with Real Estate Agents

The laws of agency have changed significantly during the last 40 years or so, and agents are no longer working just for the best interests of the seller. Today, in most states, you can work with agents who represent you the buyer, but get paid by the seller by splitting the fee with the listing agent (seller agent). Such an agent would be representing the best interests of the buyer. You can also enter into an agency whereby the agent can represent both parties in a limited agency agreement, provided both parties agree. Last, but not least, you can enter into an agency agreement whereby the agent represents you, the buyer, exclusively. Naturally, there is also an exclusive seller agency too.

Your ideal agent, known as the selling or buying agent, should think like a wholesaler rather than a retailer. When you sell a home you want a listing agent who thinks like a retailer, but not when you are buying a home, because you are looking for the very best deal. You need to qualify any agent who will be representing you to determine how hard they will work to earn your business. Trust is a two-way street. If the agent is doing a good job, then he or she deserves your loyalty, and your honesty in dealing with them.

Working with an agent opens up access to the local multiple listing services, which provide the agent with numerous possibilities to satisfy your needs. Without access to this service you will find yourself working in a more limited way, with "for sale" by owners (FSBOs), chasing down "For Sale" signs, and looking for deals through various real estate website listings.

During your search for a home, keep the following points clearly in mind:

a. Location is the most important consideration when buying real property. Any property with a view, or is close to water, or which has a larger sized lot than those in the subdivision, will bring a higher price.

b. Try to imagine what you can change to improve value. If a non-bearing wall can be knocked out to provide more living space, or there is space to later add an extra bedroom, then take note of such things. Also, cosmetic changes can make a world of difference for little cost.

c. When looking at homes in a sub-division, take note of the average prices to determine where the seller's price point should be. Is the price at the top end, in the middle, or the lower end? You always want to buy in the lower end if possible under the philosophy that a large wave raises all boats. You will experience faster appreciation that way.

d. I like to look for fixer-uppers that create the possibility of creating "sweat" equity. However, stay away from bad floor plans, and structural problems. Also remember that you will do far better in real estate if you create added value to the property. You need to get involved in the wealth creating process rather than just letting the property sit there. Otherwise, any appreciation that does take place is beyond your control, and may or may not happen.

e. Also, keep in mind that investing in real estate is similar to other investments in that you must take the time to learn your craft. Remember, you are working with large numbers, and I can't stress enough the importance of doing thorough due diligence before you make a commitment to act. The beauty is that there are plenty of people in the real estate field who are more than willing to help you: brokers, agents, lenders, title insurance employees, appraisers, home inspectors, contractors, vendors, to say nothing of the great amount of information available on the Internet as well as good books. Also, you can attend real estate classes without having to become an agent. Do it for the knowledge.

Negotiating Your Home Purchase

Understanding negotiating methods is critical in real estate if you are attempting to get the very best outcome for all your hard work. Compromises and concessions sometimes have to be made to keep the transaction going forward. It's sort of like playing chess. You sometimes have to sacrifice a pawn in order to capture a knight or a bishop, with the ultimate intention of eventually capturing the king, and coming out a winner.

Understand at the outset, that everything in real estate is negotiable: the price, terms, deposit, real estate commissions, financing, interest rates, fees, title companies, closing costs, contingencies, seller carry-backs, and buyer's final approval and walk-through. Purchasing real estate is strictly business, and should not be taken personally. I do stress the importance of always being honest in your dealings with other parties, and be sure to follow through on any commitments you make, either verbally or in writing. Also remember, that the only person you can count on in a real estate deal, to be 100% on your side, besides you, is God, (assuming you are performing according to the dictates mentioned throughout this book).

You may be asking yourself, especially if you don't particularly like to negotiate, is it worth it?

The answer clearly is a resounding yes! For instance, is it worth purchasing a home for thousands of dollars less, or selling your home for thousands of dollars more? Is it worth it to negotiate a 4% commission instead of 6%? Or, obtaining a mortgage at 4% instead of 5%? In each of these cases, there is some serious money being discussed, and you should not be thinking casually about such matters. Ask yourself how much an hour you make, and how many hours do you have to work if you negotiated a $3,000.00 savings in your favor? Always remember the old sage advice: More is always better than less; sooner is better than later, and for sure is always better than a maybe!

Here are some points you may wish to consider in your negotiations with the seller:

a. Before you negotiate you need a thorough knowledge of conditions in your market area, the sub-division you are looking at, including all closed sales, as well as current listings, and the property you are contemplating buying. Knowledge affects negotiations in every part of a real estate transaction. You also need a thorough understanding of what you and your family's needs are, as well as the reality of what a lender will loan you.

b. Always try to find out the real reason why the seller is selling. This information can sometimes reveal a high level of motivation due to a job transfer, or other reasons that could soften the seller's position when he is confronted with a lower price offer accompanied by a letter of pre-approval for your financing. Motivation is a powerful force, and can often override sound judgment, both for the seller as well as you.

c. The fewer contingencies you put in the purchase contract, the better chance you have of getting your lower price, because from the seller's point of view he is getting a clean offer with few things that could de-rail the deal. Fewer terms equals better price; lots of terms equals closer to full asking price. Everything has trade-offs.

d. Always give yourself other options. For instance, if after doing lots of shopping you come across your dream home, and you don't have another property or two to fall back on, you may end up giving the seller his full price, or more if you are in competition with another buyer. This is because your emotions might take over due to the fact that you have no other property options to fall back on if the deal does not come together. Always have options!

e. Listen very carefully to whatever you are told, take notes, and read the Book of James, chapter 3, for wisdom regarding the tongue. There is a lot of conversation that takes place before the closing, and your notebook can be a great help in resolving any issues or conflicts, especially where "material facts" are concerned. I define a material fact as anything that could affect the pocket-book of any of the parties, and therefore should be disclosed in writing to avoid future misunderstandings later on.

f. As the buyer you should be sure to include contingencies in the offering contract such as: a) subject to you obtaining successful financing; b) obtaining approval of seller's disclosure statement; c) securing approval of home inspection results, and d) signing off on a final approval of a walk-through inspection. These are what we technically refer to as contract "escape" clauses that provide the buyer with a certain level of control in making sure the sale goes as intended.

g. Finally, keep in mind that all good offers have three things in common: a) the offering price is realistic, based on solid information and facts to support your figure. A seller will at least respect your position even if he does not accept it; b) your financing arrangements must be realistic to make the seller comfortable i.e. having your lender pre-approval letter attached, and c) unless repairs are glaringly obvious and need to be addressed in the offer, you will often find that a buyer and seller may not always be fully aware of all the repairs that may need to be done at the time the offer is presented. Therefore, be sure to include your home inspection clause in the offer. In this way, rather than haggle with the seller upfront, you can make your offer look "cleaner" by tackling other repair issues later, thus increasing the chances that the seller will accept the offer.

SELLING YOUR REAL PROPERTY

If you purchase a home, the chances are high that you will one day sell it. People who buy a home and live there for the rest of their lives are rare. The good news is that selling a home is much easier than buying one. However, not everyone sells their home properly, so you need to be fully aware of the key elements of the process.

First of all, are you selling for the right reasons? Have you thought the whole process through, and explored all the issues involved, including where you are going to move to? If you are thinking of moving out of the area, you need to know the new market just as well as you know your own market, otherwise you may end up being unpleasantly surprised.

Have you thought about the tax implications of sale? As I mentioned earlier, and it is worth repeating, a married couple can avoid paying any taxes on the equity they pull out of the property up to $500,000.00, provided they have lived in their home for two of the past five-years. A single owner is limited to the first $250,000.00 of equity. Any amounts above those limits are subject to capital gains taxation. Besides tax issues, and any necessary repairs, noted below, you need to know all of the costs involved in selling your home, including real estate commission, mortgage pay-off (if applicable), escrow and title fees etc. This will allow you, after determining any repairs, to put all the numbers on paper in order to figure out just how much money you will net at escrow. Knowing these numbers in advance allows you to "play" with them to determine just how low you are willing to go on price or other terms in order to make a sale.

Have you taken the necessary steps to prepare your home for sale? The real work of selling your home actually begins long before you place it on the market. Most buyers will request a home inspection report as part of their offer, so don't wait for the results of the report to "hit you between the eyes" before you do something about it. You need to act now if you hope to get the very best price. Encourage other family members, friends, and your real estate agent to give you their opinions and ideas of what needs to be done to improve the look of your home. Do you know the "hot buttons" that will make your house sell? It could be a great kitchen, a wonderful patio and back-yard. It may be spacious bedrooms and bathrooms, or an RV entrance. Knowing and selling your "hot button" features and benefits are all part of staging your home for the highest price.

You need to gain a good understanding of what your home is worth, and working with a knowledgeable real estate agent, who knows the local market, is a good first step. Carefully study the agent's market comparables and isolate the differences between your home versus the comps regarding amenities, square footage, lot size, and curb appeal etc., to ensure you don't miss an important selling benefit.

Finally, I recommend, depending on market conditions of course, that you sell your home before you purchase another one. Yes, you could make an offer on another home contingent upon your current home selling, but from a seller's point of view, it is a problem he would prefer not to have. Consequently, a seller might easily accept someone else's offer that is "cleaner," without such a contingency, and you could lose out on a very good deal. On the other hand, with full cash out of your current home, you make a much stronger buyer in the eyes of a seller, and this should help you negotiate a better deal going forward. If you take this approach, you need to either rent back your home from the buyer, or arrange for furniture storage while camping out with other family members until your new home is ready to close.

PIGGY-BACKING YOUR WAY TO SUCCESS

Not everyone has enough down payment to purchase a $250,000.00 home with either a 20%, or a 10% down payment. Younger families, for instance, often need to shoot for a lower valued property at first, with the intent of moving to a larger, more expensive home later. So I suggest a ten-year plan, because time is on their side. They can start off by purchasing a home they can afford, which should not be more than two to three times their annual net income, and the closer to two times the better. This requires looking at condominiums, or small fixer-up properties where they have an opportunity to improve it and improve its value. After about five-years they hopefully will have accumulated some equity due to a combination of their original down payment, any accelerated mortgage principal reduction created by making extra payments, and any appreciation in the property. They can then sell their home for a larger home that will be more suitable for their life-style, which may now include children. Remember, that if you do not have a plan, then you have already arrived at your destination, because nothing will change five-years from now. Thinking about the future is not always easy for many young people, but it shows up on their doorstep one day anyway, so why not start preparing for it now so that when it does arrive you will be happy and not disappointed.

ANOTHER TECHNIQUE TO RAPIDLY INCREASE YOUR WEALTH

Not everyone is interested in acquiring rental properties, but for those of you that want to know more, I will provide a small illustration of how the use of leverage can accelerate your wealth holdings in real estate.

First, there is no difference between purchasing a single family home or a one to four unit apartment building. They are all classified as residential properties according to the government, and financing terms, and other housing rules are similar. If you purchase five or more apartments, then they are considered commercial real estate, and come under different rules and different financing terms. Therefore, we will stick to buying a four unit apartment complex, because it boosts your leverage position compared to buying a single family home, while still being classified as residential.

Let's say you purchase a four-plex apartment building for $300,000.00. You rent out three of the units for $850.00 each, and move into the fourth one yourself (this system works even if you do not move into one of the apartments, but decide to rent out all four units). With three units rented, and living in the fourth, you now have $2,550.00 per month to offset your costs. You paid out $60,000.00 (20% of the purchase price) to acquire the property, and you obtained favorable 30 year financing at 4%, with a monthly payment of $1,142.00. Your property taxes and insurance total $3,500.00 per year ($292.00 per month), and you allocate $5,000.00 a year for repairs and maintenance, which can vary depending on the age and shape of the property. Our example works out to about $417.00 per month. Your total cost amounts to $1,851.00 per month, leaving you with a surplus cash flow of $699.00 per month. Next we look at the variables. As long as the units are fully occupied you have a positive cash flow of $1,549.00 ($699.00 plus your free rent of $850.00), which is equivalent to an annual savings to you of $18,588.00. This savings will continue to rise when all three units are occupied due to future rent increases, and like the squirrel mentioned earlier, this savings helps to partially pay down the mortgage faster, while also keeping some in reserve to offset rental vacancies. If a tenant did move out, the rents would drop to $1,700.00 until re-rented. At this point your monthly cash flow becomes a negative $151.00, so in this same month you have to hypothetically pay rent on your own unit, which on paper means that you still have a positive cash flow of $699.00 (your rent of $850.00 less the $151.00 negative cash flow). In reality, you would jut pay the $151.00.

Even when two units become vacant, it is generally only for a short time if you are properly maintaining the property and keeping your rents competitive. With two units vacant, your total rents collected would be $850.00. After paying your own rent, you would only be $151.00 per month out of pocket until the units are re-rented. So your risk overall is relatively low.

Now let us explore your other benefits. First, the unit you occupy is considered a residential home, which cannot be depreciated on your tax return. The other three units can be depreciated because they are rentals. For instance, since you paid $300,000.00 for the four-plex, you must first deduct the value of the land, which cannot be depreciated. Therefore, assume the land represents 20% of the purchase price and the property improvements represent 80%. So you take $300,000.00 x .8 = $240,000.00 for the improvements, which is then divided by 27.5 years (the I.R.S. allowable depreciation schedule), equaling $8,727.00 in annual tax write-off. However, because you live in one of the units, you can only deduct 75% of the $8,727.00, giving you a personal tax write-off of $6,545.00 per year. Also remember that you qualify for a tax write-off on all the interest you paid on the mortgage, along with property insurance, repairs and capital improvements. The benefit of all these tax write-offs will, of course, depend on what tax bracket you fall into. The beauty is that the total amount of the write-offs can be deducted from other household income resulting in significant tax savings for the family.

Also, equity continues to build up each year due to principal reduction on your mortgage, based on how many extra payments you decide to pay each year, plus any capital improvements you make to the property to enhance its value, and of course, any appreciation due to normal market forces.

You also make the art of leverage work in your favor. An example would be where any annual rent increase helps boost your cash flow, which consequently creates a higher value for the property based on an earning approach to value. Also, if the property goes up 5% in value in the first year due to inflation, its new value is $315,000.00. Remember, you put $60,000.00 as a down payment, which means that you have generated a 25% cash-on-cash return on your original investment ($15,000.00/$60,000.00). What other investment could provide such a great return? This happened because inflation worked in your favor rather than against you. Interesting how leverage works, isn't it?

This chapter on purchasing real estate was provided as part of an overall plan in helping you work towards a dignified retirement. Remember that time is finite, and the quicker you get into real estate ownership, the better your chances of paying-off the mortgage before you retire. It was Kay Lyons who stated that yesterday is a cancelled check; tomorrow is a promissory note. Today is the only cash you have, so spend it wisely.

I hope that the illustrations I have presented in this chapter have provided clarity in demonstrating how rapidly a family can obtain wealth if they go about it in the right way. You always have to remember, though, that no matter how much wealth you acquire, you are only the steward of that wealth, because it all belongs to God. As long as you keep that fact in mind, and pay your tithes and giving faithfully, God will always be your partner in helping you in your quest for success.

CHAPTER THIRTEEN

INVESTING FOR RETIREMENT

When a man retires, his wife gets twice
the husband, but only half the income!
– Chi Chi Rodriguez

PRIOR TO THIS chapter, we have discussed the debt plagued issues of many American households, and how to correct the problem if you are in that position. We went through the process of creating a personal budget that the whole family can work with, and then we used the double down debt reduction method to show you how to get out of debt completely. We also discussed how the credit system works, and how you can turn it around so that you use credit wisely instead of paying absorbent interest charges. We also explored the topic of starting your own small business to accelerate wealth production, and the type of business entity suitable for your needs. Another part of our discussion involved methods and techniques that allowed you to make really smart decisions on two of the largest household expenses, transportation and real estate, which are expensive, but difficult to live without. Now we turn our attention to investing for retirement.

There was a time when investing was more simple. If you wanted to buy stocks or bonds, you called a stock broker. If you wanted to purchase real estate, you sought out a real estate agent. If you wanted insurance, you would call an insurance agent. And in those days, you needed a bank account in order to write checks.

Since deregulation of our financial industries, however, the lines have become far more blurred between financial institutions. Banks today sell life insurance and stocks; insurance companies sell mutual funds and annuities, and most of the firms on Wall Street sell a variety of investments including insurance and various types of credit, including home mortgages, as well as check cashing privileges. This de-regulation of the banking industry, unfortunately, led to a major credit crisis that finally exploded in 2008.

What goes around eventually comes around, and American banking is no different in that the original Glass-Steagall Act (1933), was implemented to place a fire-wall between commercial and investment banking, due to financial scandals on Wall Street. This prevented securities firms and investment banks from taking deposits, and commercial Federal Reserve member banks from: 1) dealing in non-governmental securities for customers, 2) investing in non-investment grade securities themselves, 3) underwriting or distributing non-governmental securities, and 4) affiliating with companies involved in such activities. This seemed prudent, but unfortunately, in 1999, President Bill Clinton signed into law the Gramm-Leach-Bliley Act (GLBA), which essentially knocked down the Glass-Steagall fire-wall, and ended up consolidating commercial banks, investment banks, insurance companies, and securities firms. This allowed investment banks to make exotic investments using customer deposits, and we later saw our financial system go into free fall, causing the loss of billions of investor funds.

So, have we learned the lessons of history, or are we doomed to repeat them? I would like to think that we are much smarter investors today, thanks to the tremendous financial history we have, that we can turn to when trying to figure out financial strategies for the future. Since 2008, for instance, we have already put in place new financial regulations, called the Dodd-Frank Wall Street Reform and Consumer Protection Act, which is designed to prevent another 2008 mistake.

The lesson for all of us, however, is to take our financial investments seriously, by learning as much as we can, and not taking unnecessary risks. As long as your investment rate of return is higher each year than the inflation rate, you should be just fine when you eventually retire.

RETIRING ON A SOCIAL SECURITY CHECK

The average Social Security check today is between $1,300.00 and $1,400.00 a month, and generally increases at about 2% per annum. It was never meant to be a complete answer to your retirement financial needs. It is subsistence, and meant primarily to provide food, clothing and shelter, perhaps covering about 40% of your monthly needs. Unfortunately 21% of retirees live solely on their Social Security check, and therefore without other sources of income, it is hard to balance most household budgets. If you are married, and one spouse does not work outside of the home, that spouse is entitled to 50% of what the working spouse collects, when eligible. Working spouses are entitled to individual benefits or half of their spouse's benefits, whichever is greater. To obtain further information you can contact the Social Security Administration by calling: 800-772-1213, and completing form 7004. The main point being expressed in this paragraph is to point out that we must start now to provide for a dignified retirement, unless we already have other sources of income in place, such as pensions, savings, or other income producing investments.

DO IT YOURSELF INVESTING (DIY), OR SEEK PROFESSIONAL HELP?

When thinking about the future, you could spend a lot of time researching and investigating all types of investment vehicles, but what about that day time job that sustains the family budget, and absorbs so much time? Surveys tell us that most people view their investments as a side line, because they are concentrating on their careers, and family life. That doesn't mean they don't take their investments seriously. It is a question of finding the time, which is precious to all of us.

What we do know is, that time waits for no man, and doing nothing about our future retirement security is not an option. Inflation, that silent killer of dollar purchasing power, has ranged from minus 15.80% to a plus of 23.70%, with an average of about 3.32% annually over the last 100 years. Recently, inflation has been below 2%. It has been estimated that if you need $50,000.00 a year today to cover your expenses, then you will need $92,000.00 in the year 2035 using a 3% inflation rate, and assuming inflation does not trend higher. Unless we expect to live an impoverished retirement, we need to start planning as soon as possible, because inflation, just like taxes and death, is a reality we all must face.

If you have the time to research your own investments, by all means do so, provided you have gained the knowledge and skills that are essential to success. On the other hand, many people have made effective use of working with an experienced financial advisor, which is what I recommend, but not before having thoroughly researched the benefits of a good paying job's 401K Retirement Plan first. If you don't have this option, then a good financial advisor is able to assess your risk tolerance, and create a custom plan to grow your funds in order to reach certain targeted goals that you have pre-set.

TYPES OF FINANCIAL ADVISORS

You have lots of choices when it comes to selecting a financial advisor to work with, which can be a little confusing. Although I do not want to recommend any one advisor over another, and space limitations does not allow me to provide you with a comprehensive list, I will mention two advisor designations that I believe you should check out before you go further with your plans. I simply want to provide you with some background information that should prove helpful to you as you make your decision.

Registered Investment Advisors: Licensed by the Securities and Exchange Commission, RIAs manage your funds in a fiduciary capacity, meaning they operate with the highest level of integrity in how they invest your funds in your best interests. They manage your account continually with the goal of reaching your objectives. They are fee based, usually charging about 1% of the total funds under management. The better they do, the more they make for themselves. It's a win-win for both parties.

Certified Financial Planners: Certified by the Certified Financial Planner Board, CFPs go through a very intense training program that covers a broad area of subjects, such as investments, insurance, taxes, and retirement planning. A CFP can be a good choice if you want someone to put together a detailed financial plan to increase your chances of enjoying a worry free retirement. They normally charge a flat fee for a plan, a percentage of assets they manage on your behalf, or a commission if you purchase certain financial products from them.

WHAT TO LOOK FOR IN A FINANCIAL ADVISOR:

I look for three things when working with a financial advisor: technical competence gained through experience; independence, and strong ethics.

Technical competence is ascertained by investigating both the education and career background of the individual in question. Finance, taxes, accounting, and law are good backgrounds for financial advisors. Industry experience should be at least five to ten years in the field, as it takes that long to effectively work as a good advisor.

Independence is another criterion, because those advisors that work for large firms are often under pressure to sell the firm's recommended products that create the largest profits for the firm. You want the advisor working for you, not for the firm. Therefore, working with a financial advisor of a smaller, private firm is a better way to go.

Strong ethics is another requirement. You can check-out a financial advisor by going to various websites such as The Securities & Exchange Commission (SEC): www.sec.gov, and the Financial Industry Regulatory Authority (FINRA), which can be reached at: www.finra.org. Both of these institutions make licensee information available to the general public, so you can search the backgrounds of brokers and investment advisors. Having no violations does not mean that the broker is ethical. Sometimes the exact opposite is true. Sometimes very ethical brokers end up in disputes that are reported by clients, but have nothing to do with a breach of ethics. In our day, there are numerous people who like to file complaints or law-suits for almost any reason. Therefore, be careful in reviewing the details of any advisor's bio.

Finding a Financial Advisor

Many people find a good financial advisor through friends, co-workers, church members, their accountant, or going to the websites mentioned above. When you meet, it is important to be prepared with a number of questions that you need solid answers to. Does the advisor meet the three criteria we just reviewed – education, career background, and ethical standards of a good fiduciary? Does he act independently from any large firm that often put their own needs above their clients? Finally, is there good chemistry between the two of you? Are you confident that you can create a long lasting, trusting and friendly relationship?

CHARACTERISTICS OF A PERFECT INVESTMENT:

I like to start out by describing the perfect investment, because it highlights and illustrates the various characteristics of a good investment. So this is what a perfect investment would look like:

a. You receive a guaranteed high rate of return, which pays twice the rate of inflation.

b. All your principal investment is 100% guaranteed by the federal government.

c. You are provided with great potential for the growth of your investment.

d. The investment is 100% liquid, allowing you to convert to cash at any time.

e. Any earnings from the investment are fully protected from all forms of taxes.

f. It will also take out the trash! (I think you can eliminate this one!).

Those are the character traits we look for in a perfect world, but in a fallen world we have to settle for less. It's possible to find investments with at least one, up to perhaps three of the above traits, which causes risk to enter the picture. Then we must deal with the risk/reward equation.

"LENDING" VERSUS "OWNING" INVESTMENTS

Generally, there are only two ways to invest your money. You can lend it to someone, or you can buy something with it. You are lending your money when you buy government bonds, place it in a CD, savings account, or when you purchase a corporate bond. However, when you buy a share of common stock, or invest in real estate, gold, silver, or other commodities, you become a part or full owner. Lending your money usually provides less risk compared with buying something. Lenders of money do face another type of risk, however. If you purchase a bond that yields 4%, and interest rates rise above 4%, or inflation suddenly jumps to 10%, the value of your bond holding diminishes in value. When you become an owner of the investment, you benefit from a rise in inflation, which is a good thing. However, when you own you also find that your cash flow is not protected. The value could rise rapidly, or it could drop rapidly, and you have no control over market forces. Generally speaking, however, when you own something, which creates equity such as stocks or real estate, you will find, in the long run, that they usually out-perform investments where you are lending your money.

TYPES OF "LENDING" INVESTMENTS

The following information is provided to acquaint you with various types of investments so that when you sit down with a financial advisor, you will at least have a basic rudimentary understanding of the fundamental differences between each type. Once you have a good understanding of the pros and cons of each type of investment, it should provide you with more confidence when you put together, with the help of your advisor, a financial plan that takes into consideration your risk profile, as well as the goals you set for yourself. So let's start with "lending" investments.

U.S. TREASURY SECURITIES:

These investments are a direct obligation of the federal government, and they represent the gold standard for safety both here, and around the world. There are several types:

Treasury Bills: They are issued in minimum denominations of $1,000.00, and expire in a year or less. There is no stated interest. Instead, they are sold at auction for less than their "face" value (that is for less than $1,000.00 in the above case). When they come due, their full face value is paid out i.e. the full $1,000.00. For instance, you may pay $990.00 for a T-bill and then receive the full $1,000.00 when it matures three-months later.

Treasury Notes: Issued in minimums of $1,000.00, they mature in one to ten-years. They provide a stated interest, which is paid semi-annually. T-Notes are also sold through auction, and can be purchased for more or less than their stated face value, depending on current interest rates.

Treasury Bonds: They are very similar to notes, with the exception that they mature in more than ten-years. You can buy them at auction directly from the federal government, or from a stock broker, or your financial advisor. U.S. savings bonds have been popular for years, and they are purchased at a discount from face value, similar to zero coupon bonds. Federal taxes are not paid until the bond is cashed in, and state and local taxes are generally exempt. There are other types of bonds issued by federal agencies such as the Federal Home Loan Bank, and government sponsored enterprises such as Fannie Mae. They are considered one step removed from our government, but are considered quite safe nonetheless.

CERTIFICATES OF DEPOSIT:

Traditionally provided by the banking industry, CDs are guaranteed by the Federal Deposit Insurance Corporation (FDIC). In other words they are guaranteed by the full faith of the United State government up to $250,000.00 per banking institution. Therefore, any amounts above this figure should be invested in other banks to gain full protection. CDs have worked well for a long time as a safe harbor for parking your funds, and the longer the contract time commitment, the higher the interest rate. That is why many investors have chosen to "ladder" their CD investments by placing funds in short, medium and longer time periods to boost an overall higher yield on their total investment, while at the same time having the opportunity to pull money out periodically, without penalty. Unfortunately, in recent years, the rates of return have been lower than the rate of inflation, which makes them a poor investment. Therefore, only use CDs as a temporary holding place for surplus funds until you can find a higher yielding investment. The one exception I am aware of is to invest in CDs that are tied into the Standard & Poor's 500 Stock Index, which provides an opportunity to invest in the stock market without taking any risk.

CORPORATE BONDS:

When you loan money to a private corporation, they pay a fixed rate of return every six-months, for a time period of ten, twenty or thirty years. The longer the time-frame to pay-off the bond, the higher the rate of return. When contemplating a corporate bond investment, it is not necessary to check-out the finances of the corporation in question. Bond rating agencies, such as Moody's, Standard & Poor's, Fitch, and Kroll Bond Ratings, provide widely used letter grades to determine risk. "Junk" Bonds, for instance, are rated BB or lower. Below are the letter grades.

I should also explain that there is a difference between a bond that is backed by a specific asset of the corporation, which decreases the bond holder's risk, versus a debenture, which is backed only by the corporation's reputation and credit worthiness, and is the more common of the two. Corporate bonds in general, usually pay a higher return than short term investments, like money market funds, long term treasury securities, or certificates of deposit. They can be purchased directly, or you can purchase them through mutual funds, and unit investment trusts (discussed later).

Rating Category	Ratings Symbols	Rating Notches
Exceptional	AAA	-
Superior	AA	AA+, AA-
Excellent	A	A+, A-
Good	BBB	BBB+, BBB-
Fair	BB	BB+, BB-
Marginal	B	B+, B-
Weak	CCC	CCC+, CCC-
Very Weak	CC	-
Poor	C	-

Convertible Bonds: Some corporate bonds are convertible, meaning they can be exchanged for a specific number of shares of common stock, which by proxy allows them to participate in any growth in the stock value. Unfortunately, because of the benefits of conversion, they generally pay lower rates of return.

Municipal Bonds: These types of bonds are issued by local governments, such as cities or states, and offer the feature of being free of federal taxes, and also free of state taxes if purchased by residents in the state where they are issued. This feature makes muni-bonds highly appealing to people who are in a high tax bracket. For instance, if you are in a 28% tax bracket, and you purchase a muni-bond paying 5%, it is worth nearly as much as a corporate bond paying nearly 7%. If you choose this type of investment, be sure not to put them inside a 401K plan, because 401K plans are automatically exempt from taxes until you are about to retire, and ready to use the funds.

Mortgage Backed Securities: These are generally safe investments, and can be purchased by individual investors. The Government National Mortgage Association (GNMA), buys federally insured mortgages from banks and other lending institutions, then puts them into pools consisting of thousands of mortgages, and then sells shares in theses pools. Each investor then receives a proportional share of the principal and interest payments made on those mortgages. The smallest unit sold by GNMA costs $25,000.00, but investors can purchase directly for as little as $1,000.00 inside a GNMA mutual fund or unit trust.

International Bonds: All foreign bonds must meet the same standards of disclosure as any domestic bond underwriting, and pay out in U.S. dollars. They are typically rated by our bonding agencies mentioned earlier. With one call to your broker, you can purchase British, French or German bonds, that generally pay a higher rate than domestic issues. The main concern is currency exchange rates, which could either increase or decrease your rate of return. A good reason to consider international investments in general, is to know that American equities have dropped considerably since 1970, when the U.S. equity market capitalization represented 66% of the global cap rate. By 1999 it had dropped to 50%, and today it represents about 37% of the world cap rate of $61.9 trillion. Therefore, almost two-thirds of equity investments now lie outside the U.S., meaning you could be losing out on some good opportunities.

TYPES OF EQUITY OR "OWNING" INVESTMENTS

If you are willing to take more risk, you can capitalize on increases in future inflation, and by exercising the power of leverage. This allows for the possibility of allowing your investments to grow faster by owning an asset rather than lending your money at interest. Remember, you have limited time to plan for retirement, maybe 40 years or much less. Therefore, investment vehicles that accelerate your wealth position are the type of investments well worth looking at.

STOCKS: Stocks go up and stocks go down, but in the long run, according to Morningstar, the American stock market has averaged 10.4% annual return before inflation, since 1900, which is far better than any fixed income investment.

At the very least, stocks generally trend with inflation, which generally rises every year, causing the products that company's sell, such as toothpaste, shampoo, energy etc., to also increase in value. Many products created by corporations are consumable and need to be replaced often, thus providing a continual stream of profits. Upon further review you will also find that American corporations have done a fantastic job of tapping into new technology, and innovative ways of making things better.

One way of determining corporate wealth is known as return on equity, which is the corporation's net worth (difference between assets and liabilities). The average return on equity over the last 80 years has been about 10%. Therefore, it is no coincidence that on average, the stock of those corporations has appreciated at about the same rate.

Although stocks have the potential to provide greater rates of return compared to other investments, nonetheless there is risk involved. Therefore, stock investments should not be taken lightly. If you are young, you have plenty of time to recuperate when stocks decrease in value, but older investors have less time.

So, with these thoughts in mind, let us look at some strategies you can take to reduce your risk, with the understanding that limited space does not allow me to provide a more comprehensive review of stock investments, but we can at least get you started in the right direction.

A "Bull" market is one that is rising in value. A "Bear" market is one that decreases in value at least 20% from its 52 week high. Between 1900 and 2008, we have experienced 32 Bear markets, and the average duration has been about 367 days, but conventional wisdom likes to say about 18 months. The 20% drop is based on stock indices such as the Dow Jones Industrial Average, the S&P 500, and NASAQ.

If you do decide to purchase stocks on your own, rather than through a financial advisor, I would advise not to try to "time" the market unless you are well informed and have lots of experience. Many large stock market gains happen without notice, and you could be in cash when they happen. Therefore, it may be more advisable when you purchase stock to place a stop loss on the stock that triggers a market order to sell if the stock price dips to a lower, specific value than what you paid. By doing this, you gain in the sense that you avoid a Bear market drop, while at the same time benefiting while the stock continues to rise, by adjusting your stop loss position to a higher number as your stock increases in value. The idea is to prevent big losses, while trying to capitalize on any gains. If the stock value drops, your stop order will automatically sell you out. In some cases you may lose a little, plus some brokerage fees, but often you are sold out after the stock has risen, creating a gain for you. By using an Internet discount brokerage house, your fees are minimal compared to the past before the Internet came along.

Keep in mind, however, that when you buy a few stocks, you have no diversity to spread the risk. There are eleven sectors in our economy; some go up and some go down. By spreading your stock investments across economic sectors, you increase the odds in your favor that if one sector drops, another will rise. Of course, if you want good diversification, you can always invest in a stock mutual fund, which we will discuss later. For the record, here are the sectors:

Market Capitalization (trillions)			
Consumer Discretionary	$4.61	Industrials	$3.62
Consumer Staples	$3.79	Info Technology	$6.88
Energy	$3.47	Materials	$1.85
Financials	$6.64	Real Estate	$1.13
Health Care	$4.51	Telecommunications	$1.82
Utilities	$1.15		
			2016

The Common Sense Factor: Selecting a company to invest in takes common sense, not financial genius. You want to invest in a firm that is honest, with effective management, and is creating a product or service that people want. Products and services should be sold at an attractive price, and very importantly it should demonstrate mastery of the steps involved between the creation of the product or service, and its ultimate delivery to the customer. You want a company that knows how to deal with complexity, and should be able to quickly adapt to change. Firms that have good research and development departments help them to stay on the "cutting edge" of new innovations in their industries. Last but not least, the firm should have its financial house in order. Your advisor should have plenty of such firms to bring to your attention, aided with lots of research, and backed up with detailed analysis.

Blue Chip Stocks: One option you have is to invest in so called "blue chip" stocks. These are stocks that represent the strongest stocks, and include companies with long track records of success, and are often included in the DOW 30 (the Dow Jones Industrial average, made up of the 30 top stocks on the Standard & Poor's rating index). They include companies like: Johnson & Johnson, IBM, McDonalds, Pfizer, Proctor & Gamble, Verizon, 3M, and Merck, for example. Blue Chip companies are so large, so well entrenched in their respective markets, and so integrated into the American economy, they are sure to be around as long as the U.S. is.

Americans are so used to buying their products: toothpaste, baby diapers, hamburgers, creams etc., (many that need to be constantly replenished), it almost becomes a foregone assumption that sales volume will be there next year, and the year after. Investments in Blue Chip stocks are no way to get rich quick, but they do represent a good opportunity, in the long run, to provide you with a rate of return, including dividends, above inflation rates as you work towards retirement. So, if you can find firms that are able to achieve steady and moderate growth year after year, using the average rate of 10%, it is clear that by using the rule of 72 mentioned earlier, a 10% return would double your invest every 7.2 years. Personally, in the current market I would be happy with less, because inflation has been kept under control now for some time.

MUTUAL FUNDS:

A mutual fund is an investment pool that allows large and small investors alike to buy shares. The monies are used to maintain a portfolio of investments that could include hundreds of stocks, bonds and other types of investments. A review of the fund's prospectus will describe their investment philosophy, and what they are trying to accomplish. The large majority of funds are "open-ended" funds, meaning they will create new shares for new investors. The trading price is called the net asset value (NAV), or the market value of the fund's investments divided by the number of shares outstanding. There are also "closed-end" funds, which issue a specific number of shares, and new investors can only get into the fund if an existing fund investor wishes to sell out.

Mutual funds first came into existence during the 1920s, but did not hit their stride until the last 50 years or so. By the end of 2015 there were more than 9,000 mutual funds in the U.S. with assets totaling $15.65 trillion. Around the world, as of the end of 2014, there were more than 79,000 mutual funds! This information provides you with some perspective of the huge size and scope of the mutual fund industry. There are mutual funds that invest in almost any asset that you could purchase directly. Some funds specialize in money markets, others in pure stock plays. Yet others provide high dividends, or long term growth, or income and growth. Some funds are a hybrid between stocks and bonds, and yet others concentrate on small, high risk firms. You can also find funds that specialize in gold, silver, other precious metals, and even funds that are into high-tech foreign companies, especially emerging markets. The bottom line is that there are a multitude of funds to choose from depending on your investment style and goals.

Some of the benefits of investing in mutual funds are that, unlike single stock plays, they offer diversity by spreading risk over a large number of individual companies. They also offer professional management. While you may only be spending a few minutes a day trying to analyze the stock market, professional fund managers, along with their staff, aided with access to numerous sources of information (that an individual investor may not have available), are working around the clock to provide the best performance possible. A third benefit mutual funds offer, is easy access for small investors to get into the funding pool. Yet another benefit is the convenience mutual funds provide by handling all the bookkeeping requirements. They also provide automatic deposit privileges so that you can invest every month if you wish. Also, exiting from the fund requires a simple phone call to sell, making them highly liquid.

Mutual Fund Fees:

One of the disadvantages of investing in mutual funds are the fees charged, which you need to check carefully as they fluctuate from one fund to another. According to the Investment Company Institute, the average expense ratio in an equity mutual fund is 1.4% per year. This is average, meaning that many are higher, especially in small funds where there is a smaller investor base to leverage the funds costs. However, unstated expenses are more difficult to verify because they are factored on several variables, and are not required by law to be disclosed. The stated costs include administrative fees, management fees, marketing fees, and load fees (explained in a moment). However, the unstated fees include trading costs, commissions, market impact costs, and taxes. Therefore, you need to discuss this issue with your advisor before you make the investment.

One last point. Mutual funds are generally categorized as A, B or C shares. The A shares are front loaded, meaning that a sales fee is deducted immediately from your invested funds. B shares have no upfront sales fee, but expense fees are generally higher than A shares. Thirdly, C shares have no upfront sales charge, but they may charge 1% if sold within one-year. Also, expense fees are usually higher than A and B shares. Consult your advisor for more information.

UNIT INVESTMENT TRUSTS:

Similar to mutual funds, Unit Investment Trusts contain a portfolio of securities analyzed and put together by financial professionals. Shares, or units, can then be purchased by the public. Unlike a mutual fund where investments are continually adjusted, UIT investments are not generally changed for the life of the trust, which is generally about one or two years. They, like mutual funds, offer diversification, easy accessibility, and convenience. The buy and hold nature of UITs is preferred by some investors who want to know what they own, and will not constantly change due to lots of sales activity.

ANNUITIES

This investment product is created by insurance companies, and generally marketed by them or securities brokers. There is no annual limit regarding how much you invest, and they provide similar tax advantages to a 401K, and other retirement plans. Annuities are another form of retirement strategy, and can provide a variety of benefits including growth, tax-free income, market upside without the downside risk, and income for life.

There are generally four kinds of annuities: immediate, fixed, variable, and fixed index. You can receive immediate regular income from an Immediate Annuity for your lifetime. It can be a good supplement for Social Security, especially if you do not have a pension plan. Once the money is in, you can't pull it out without substantial penalty. With a Fixed Annuity, you earn a steady rate of return, between 1% and 4%, for a fixed period of time. The longer the annuity is extended, the higher the earnings percentage. Variable Annuities are tied to the stock market, which means you have the potential for substantial growth, or suffer losses. Fees generally run between 2% to 8%, so it is important to study the details of any contract you sign. Variable annuities are typically not recommended as a retirement strategy. Finally, there are Fixed Indexed Annuities, which provide features of both fixed and variable annuities. If the chosen market index goes up, you participate in some or all of the gain, depending on whether there is a top side cap. However, if the market goes down, you don't lose money.

There are a number of moving parts associated with annuity investing, and I highly recommend you work with a retirement specialist who understands the many annuity products on the market before proceeding with an annuity purchase. Also, remember that there is a hefty sales commission to whoever sells you an annuity, so be sure to be comfortable with whoever you do business with. Notwithstanding what I have just said, the annuity industry continues to grow, with total annual sales of $5.25 billion in the year 2000, climbing to $74 billion at the end of 2014.

REAL ESTATE INVESTMENT TRUST (REITS)

REITs are similar to mutual funds in that they receive funds from investors, but instead of investing in stocks and bonds, they invest in buildings. REITs purchase buildings, as well as make mortgage loans on buildings, and some have both debt and equity positions in real estate. You can purchase REIT shares just like stocks as they are listed on stock exchanges. Like mutual funds, REITs provide diversification and professional management. It is a liquid asset in that, although REITs invest in real estate, your shares can be sold for cash almost immediately.

MASTER LIMITED PARTNERSHIPS (MLPs)

MLPs are publicly traded partnerships, which have been around since the early 1980s. They mainly invest in the energy industry, although some invest in the financial markets as well. There are two types of partners: the general partner who makes the day-to-day decisions, and limited partners, who invest their money. Limited partners are able to take a percentage of the MLPs depreciation schedule, because MLPs pay no federal taxes due to being a pass-through entity for tax purposes. MLPs must earn at least 90% of their gross income from qualified sources, with distribution of profits made every quarter. Generally, the higher the distribution, the higher the management fee paid to the general partner. This creates an incentive for the general partner to perform well.

PRECIOUS METALS

Precious metals, particularly gold and silver, are popular investments during times of high inflation, because commodities increase in value as the inflation rate rises. Gold has some special characteristics because it has been used as a form of money for centuries. People like gold because it is scarce, transportable, divisible, and nonperishable. It is also a highly liquid product that can be sold anywhere in the world. It is a great source of wealth to people living in countries where there is economic or political instability. In a way, you could make the case that people who purchase gold are betting on future uncertainty that will rock the markets and cause gold to rise in value. You can purchase gold in a number of forms: gold bullion bars, gold bullion coins issued by the United States, Canada, China, and other countries, like South Africa, or stock in gold mining companies or mutual funds that invest in that type of company. You can also purchase gold through precious metal mutual funds or managed portfolios, as well as gold futures.

Perhaps the main negative in owning gold is the fact that after you have purchased some, it just sits there. It is not involved in the wealth creating process, and it doesn't pay interest or dividends. You also have storage and insurance costs. So, unless the Four Horsemen of the Apocalypse don't come running through your city, you may find that an investment in gold denies you the opportunity cost of investing in something that could give you a better return. Nonetheless, it is probably not a bad idea to have some of your money invested in gold, silver, or other precious metals, but I would not recommend more than 5% or 10% maximum of your total asset value.

COLLECTIBLES

Collectibles include paintings, antiques, rare coins, stamps and even comic books. Some people have made a lot of money specializing in a particular collectible area, such as a van Gogh 19th century painting that sold for more than $40 million! Others have done well trading in classic automobiles, and one friend of mine actually makes a living buying and selling rare coins from his home. However, for every success story, there are plenty of people who end up with paintings on their walls, and coins that lie in dusty cupboards. The key is not to purchase a collectible as an investment, unless you can enjoy having them hanging on the wall, or sitting in a display case to show to friends. Intensive research is key.

In this chapter we have discussed most of the major types of investments, with the exception of real estate, which was mentioned in the last chapter. I have deliberately stayed away from the more exotic types of investments such as foreign currency, futures, and option trading due to the larger risks involved. The basic fundamentals of each investment mentioned, should provide you with a good understanding when you sit down with your financial professional to discuss your various options. Your risk tolerance level should be evaluated in allocating your investments among different investment strategies. The goal is to earn a good rate of return, higher than inflation, while also paying careful attention to risk. We can control the controllables in our life, but we cannot control the uncontrollables. Therefore, we need to use all the "tools" available to us to get the job done, and earn a good retirement. This means doing your own research, working with a professional financial advisor, and making a binding investment with God who will guide you through troubled waters.

RETIREMENT TIPS

1. Start your family budget, get out of debt, and clean up your credit profile.

2. Start a savings plan. It is easier to live below your means while you are working and bringing home a salary, than when living on investment income. Remember, a social security check will cover, on average, about 40% of your income needs in retirement.

3. If your employer matches any 401K contributions, take full advantage.

4. Select a good financial advisor using the guidelines mentioned earlier.

5. Draw up a will and change it periodically to fit your new circumstances.

6. You might also consider setting up a Revocable Living Trust to avoid probate costs upon death. We will discuss this subject later.

7. Plan for a very long life. Life expectancy levels are changing. The average age of death in 1952 was 68.6 years; in 2006 it was 77.8 years. Today, if you are age 65, you could live until you are 90!

8. Calculate inflation into your future planning. This is often overlooked.

9. Involve your spouse and kids in your financial decisions and goals. Make it a team effort.

10. Get a good tax advisor whose fee will be returned many times over with tax savings.

11. Review your asset allocation regularly to adjust to the current and long term reality.

12. If you have a low paying job, think seriously about starting your own home business.

13. Review your insurance policies annually: life, disability, health, and long term care.

14. Plan to pay-off your mortgage before you retire. You can thank me later.

15. While you are doing these things, be sure to have some fun along the way!

We have covered a great deal of material in this chapter (as we probably did in all chapters), and therefore I don't want you to feel overwhelmed. As the circus master once asked, "How do you eat an elephant?" The answer is one bite at a time. Therefore, now that you own this book, you can use it like any other resource material, like a dictionary or an encyclopedia, by simply selecting subjects individually for study. In this way, you will over time, consume the whole elephant (figuratively speaking). Remember also that people go to university for four years to study similar material, so don't be dismayed if you spend six months digesting the material, and doing further research. There is no doubt in my mind that your increased earnings and savings, over the long term, will more than adequately compensate you for the time you spend increasing your knowledge of money management.

CHAPTER FOURTEEN

ESTATE PLANNING AND ASSET PROTECTION

There are known knowns, these are knowns that
we know that we know. There are also known
unknowns. These are knowns that we know that
we don't know. Also, there are unknown unknowns.
These are the unknowns that we don't know
that we don't know!

– Donald Rumsfeld

WE HAVE TRAVELED a long way since the first chapter, and by following the strategies laid out, many of you are perhaps now thinking more seriously about your own retirement situation. There are lots of unknowns out there, but there are also facts that we can be certain of, such as experiencing a poor retirement lifestyle if we don't start planning for it now. Not having a vision and goal for the future can lead to all types of problems. Here are a few examples:

1. You become disabled and are unable to manage your finances. Part of your planning should perhaps include disability insurance, and also a power of attorney designating who will take control of your assets, should you become incompetent.

2. Imagine if you die and you have not named a guardian for your children, which forces the courts to make the decision for you.

3. Suppose you get sued, and a large judgment is imposed against you. A good estate plan could include strategies that could protect many of your assets.

4. Your children inherit a lot of money at an age that could destroy their ambition and work ethic in establishing their own independence.

5. You or your spouse move to a nursing home and the bills consume all your assets, because you had not taken out long term health care insurance.

6. You fail to provide for a child with a disability or special needs.

These are just a few scenarios that are realistic possibilities for some people. The point being made is that not to plan is not an option. Of course, some younger people might make the comment that an estate plan is not necessary because they have plenty of time to do it later. They don't realize that time is their greatest advantage. By starting young, their financial journey and retirement goals are much easier to reach. The longer they wait the harder it becomes.

Some people may be avoiding estate planning because it causes them to think about death, or the death of someone they love. Unfortunately, we all must deal with death, as well as many living issues that are also very important.

SETTING ESTATE PLANNING GOALS

It is important to prioritize your goals and objectives so that you can customize a plan to meet your specific needs. Some goals may include:

- Protecting assets from your creditors

- Providing for your family
- Designating gifts to charity
- Protecting real estate ownership
- Minimizing estate and income tax
- Avoiding probate, and minimizing expenses and delays
- Dividing your assets to your beneficiaries fairly
- Keeping your financial affairs private

WORKING WITH A RETIREMENT ADVISOR

You may want to consider consulting with someone who specializes in retirement strategies, someone who can create a viable plan, and understands the need for asset protection. Here is a short list:

- Certified Public Accountants (CPAs)
- Certified Financial Planners (CFPs)
- Accredited Estate Planner (EEP)
- Estate Planning Law Specialist (EPLS)
- Chartered Financial Analyst (CFA)

PLANNING STEPS FOR YOUR FUTURE RETIREMENT

Before making an appointment with an advisor, you should take advantage of the following nine-step retirement plan that will provide you with a good "ball-park" idea of what your income needs will be when you do retire. Then, when you have completed the steps, you can work with a professional who will fine tune your numbers, if you think appropriate, and ensure that you have accounted for as many scenarios as possible. So here is a self-help approach that should provide you with a clear glimpse into your financial future. It costs you nothing, other than your time:

Step One - Organize Your Documents:

This potentially could include some or all of the following:

a. Federal and State tax returns for the last five-years

b. Two or three of your latest pay stubs (include spouse if working)

c. Current personal financial statement (Total assets minus all liabilities)

d. Current statements from brokerage and mutual fund accounts etc.

e. Retirement plan statements (401K, IRA, Keogh, pension etc.)

f. Any insurance policies (life, disability, health, property and casualty etc.)

g. Wills, trust agreements

h. Bank accounts for the last twelve months

i. Mortgages and notes payable for the last twelve months

j. Credit Card statements for the last twelve months

k. Loan agreements

Step Two- Determine Your Age of Retirement:

For illustrative purposes, in this example we will keep the process simple by assuming you are currently 40 years of age, and you wish to retire at age 65 (currently the average age for male retirement is 64). Keep in mind of course, that full eligibility for Social Security benefits will come at a later age, but for our purposes we will use the age of 65 for your target retirement age.

You can always tweak your own personal situation later. As a general rule you should figure spending about 80% in retirement of what you spend each month while you are working. Yes, in retirement you may have your mortgage paid off, and your kids are all gone, but you have more time to travel and adopt hobbies, thus increasing expenses in those categories. Therefore, we will work with 80%.

Step Three – Assessing Living Expenses:

First, complete the Worksheet furnished below using the numbers from your own personal budget figures in chapter five. For this exercise, I will be using $62,500.00 for total expenses, and $50,000.00 (80% of what will be needed in retirement). This is a nice round number to work with. Your numbers, of course, will need to be as realistic for your household as possible.

The Worksheet requires you to provide actual figures of what you are spending today, and place them in the left column. You then need to put figures in the right column that represent your best assessment, using today's dollar values, of how much you will need in retirement based on your lifestyle and spending requirements at that time. For instance, if you intend to have your home paid for, then you would place zero for home mortgage. All of the other numbers will be adjusted for inflation in a moment for the years up to retirement. Meanwhile, in the far right column you need to answer "yes" or "no" regarding any increases or decreases in the line item expenses. Naturally, you are making certain assumptions that will require adjustments in the future. Therefore, you will need to revisit your Worksheet at least once a year in order to stay on a realistic track. This exercise is going to provide you with a blueprint that will not only guide you now, but act as a "roadmap" to track your future progress.

The Worksheet:

	Estimated Current Expenses	Retirement Expenses (Today's Dollars)	Increase or Decrease in Expenses?
Contributions	$	$	
Savings	$	$	
Food at Home	$	$	
Food – Outside Home	$	$	
Home Mortgage	$	$	
Property Insurance	$	$	
Property Taxes	$	$	
All Utilities	$	$	
Phones	$	$	
Cable TV	$	$	
Alarm System	$	$	
Medical Insurance	$	$	
Clothing	$	$	
Gifts	$	$	
Auto Debt	$	$	
Other Loans	$	$	
Credit Card Debts	$	$	
Income Taxes	$	$	
Other	$	$	
Other	$	$	
TOTAL	$62,500.00	$50,000.00 (80% of $62,500.00)	

Step Four – Pre-Retirement Rates of Return:

As a general rule, people who are still working invest their funds in a more aggressive way than when they are retired. They continue to re-invest all their earned interest, dividends and capital gains. After retirement, there is greater emphasis on protecting principal. For qualified retirement accounts, IRAs, life insurance policies, and tax-deferred annuities, you calculate your rate of return on the gross rate, whereas, for personal investments you should figure the net rate of return after taxes. Historically, you should expect equity investments such as stocks and real estate to provide a return of 7 to 10 percent per annum. Fixed income investments, such as bonds, return 3 to 5 percent, and CDs and Money Market accounts have produced less than the 3 percent inflation rate in recent years.

Step Five – Estimate the Future Inflation Rate:

Using a 3% inflation rate is about average, but some people use a higher rate. Therefore, you need to choose whatever rate you feel comfortable with, but I would not recommend going over 5 percent, realizing that you will have to adjust your figures from time to time anyway.

Step Six – Determine Your Retirement Income Needs:

In this step we now take the $50,000.00 retirement expenses from the right hand column of the Worksheet in today's dollars, and multiply the figure by the inflation multiplier rate found in Table 1 below. By taking the inflation rate of 3 percent, and multiplying by the remaining years to retirement, you will have an annual retirement figure you need to live on. With 25 years to retirement, the inflation multiplier would be 2.09. Let us now take the retirement figure in the right column of the worksheet of $50,000, and after adjusting for inflation the figure becomes $104,500.00.

Step Seven – Subtract any Sources of Retirement Income:

Now we take your annual Social Security amount and subtract it from the above figure of $104,500.00. If you are not retired yet, you can obtain your estimated Social Security amount from contacting SSA direct, and they will send you an estimate of what you will be receiving based on your funding so far. You can either call them at: 800-772-1213, or you can request the information on-line at: www.ssa.gov/mystatement. Remember that their estimated number does not account for inflation, so you will need to adjust for that. In recent times, SSA checks have increased annually at just over 2%. So, 25 years at a 2% annual increase provides a factor of 1.64. Therefore, if the estimate you obtain indicates an annual SSA amount of $30,000.00, then you multiply this figure by 1.64, which gives you a figure of $49,200.00. When you subtract this figure from $104,500.00, you have a net figure of $55,300.00. If you are also fortunate to have a company pension, then you would adjust the pension amount for inflation, and then subtract it, along with your SSA money, from the $104,500.00 amount. For the moment, we will assume no pension, so you have a figure of $55,300.00 as the amount of income you will need 25 years from now to cover your expenses, so you can maintain your normal lifestyle.

Step Eight – Determine Your Retirement Fund Withdrawal Rate:

In the financial world, the consensus of opinion is to keep your annual withdrawal rate at no more than 4% of your total retirement portfolio. By limiting yourself to no more than 4% per annum, you should not run out of money before you run out of life. If you withdraw more than 4% you do take the risk that you could deplete your portfolio, which we want to avoid.

Step Nine – Determining the Amount of Investment Portfolio You will Need:

Here we simply take the $55,300.00 needed to live during our first year of retirement, 25 years from now, and divide this number by the 4% annual withdrawal rate mentioned in Step eight.

This provides you with a figure of $1,382,500.00 needed for your retirement portfolio. Let's work the numbers backwards to see how it all fits. If you have $1,382,500.00 in your investment portfolio 25 years from now, and if you take out an average of 4% per annum for living costs after you retire, that figure will be $55,300.00, which we then add to your SSA check of $49,200.00, to give us a number of $104,500.00.

At an annual withdrawal rate of 4% your financial portfolio should last you 25 years. This is easily determined by taking $1,382,500.00 and dividing by $55,300.00 = 25. If we have to take more than 4% out per annum, then the numbers look like this:

$55,300.00/5%	=	$1,106,000.00/$55,300.00	=	20 years
$55,300.00/6%	=	$ 921,667.00/$55,300.00	=	16+ years
$55,300.00/7%	=	$ 790,000.00/$55,300.00	=	14+ years

By doing this calculation you are able to better determine the kind of odds you are up against. If you are in superb health, for instance, you could live into your 90s, which would require a larger financial portfolio, or you need to live on less income. Remember, however, that you will have your social security and pension checks beyond the above years, up until you go to the Lord.

At the very least, you should be striving for a retirement where you have a free and clear home, your monthly social security check, and as much investment income as you can acquire to make your retirement as comfortable as possible.

ALREADY RETIRED?

If you are already retired, or getting close to it, you should already know what your retirement portfolio balance is, along with your

SSA check and pension amounts. Therefore, you can skip a lot of the aforementioned steps, because your only concern is ensuring you do not run out of money before you move on to heaven. Therefore, you probably have a number of different assets providing you with different rates of return. So you can either figure out the rate of return for each individual investment, or lump them altogether and assign a generic across the board rate of return for the purpose of calculating your annual rate of return. Figuring the rate of return on each individual asset is a more accurate way to go, but it takes a little more work. When you have determined the total annual amount of return expressed in dollars, you can then determine how short you are from balancing your living needs. If, for example, you need to withdraw $30,000.00 per year from your investments to add to your SSA check and pension, in order to meet your personal budget needs, then it becomes a simple case of ensuring that the $30,000.00 represents no more than 4% of your total investment value. By using this simple technique, you should be able to take any worries out of your mind, and enjoy your retirement.

I realize that this exercise is a sobering experience, but it is grounded in reality. No one wants to become a burden to their family, friends, or the government. That is why I am providing you with a road-map for your financial future, so that you still have the time to do something about it, rather than do nothing and accept the potential consequences of living in hardship after your working years are over. The days of guaranteed company pensions are gone, and SSA is not enough to cover your retirement expenses. So, unless you have rich relatives, you need to start the retirement process now, because it is biblical to be responsible with the assets God has temporarily given you stewardship over. By using the biblical principles laid out in this book, you can enjoy a financially secure future for yourself and your family, while also helping the downtrodden, the widows, the orphans, and the poorest of the poor. Furthermore, the more we prosper in the future, the more we should be thanking God each day for our many blessings.

ESTIMATED INFLATION RATE

Years until Retirement	1%	2%	3%	4%	5%	6%	7%	8%
1	1.01	1.02	1.03	1.04	1.05	1.06	1.07	1.08
2	1.02	1.04	1.06	1.08	1.10	1.12	1.14	1.17
3	1.03	1.06	1.09	1.12	1.16	1.19	1.23	1.26
4	1.04	1.08	1.13	1.17	1.22	1.26	1.31	1.36
5	1.05	1.10	1.16	1.22	1.28	1.34	1.40	1.47
6	1.06	1.13	1.19	1.27	1.34	1.42	1.50	1.59
7	1.07	1.15	1.23	1.32	1.41	1.50	1.61	1.71
8	1.08	1.17	1.27	1.37	1.48	1.59	1.72	1.85
9	1.09	1.20	1.30	1.42	1.55	1.69	1.84	2.00
10	1.10	1.22	1.34	1.48	1.63	1.79	1.97	2.16
11	1.12	1.24	1.38	1.54	1.71	1.90	2.10	2.33
12	1.13	1.27	1.43	1.60	1.80	2.01	2.25	2.52
13	1.14	1.29	1.47	1.67	1.89	2.13	2.41	2.72
14	1.15	1.32	1.51	1.73	1.98	2.26	2.58	2.94
15	1.16	1.35	1.56	1.80	2.08	2.40	2.76	3.17
16	1.17	1.37	1.60	1.87	2.18	2.54	2.95	3.43
17	1.18	1.40	1.65	1.95	2.29	2.69	3.16	3.70
18	1.20	1.43	1.70	2.03	2.41	2.85	3.38	4.00
19	1.21	1.46	1.75	2.11	2.53	3.03	3.62	4.32
20	1.22	1.49	1.81	2.19	2.65	3.21	3.87	4.66
21	1.23	1.52	1.86	2.28	2.79	3.40	4.14	5.03
22	1.24	1.55	1.92	2.37	2.93	3.60	4.43	5.44
23	1.26	1.58	1.97	2.46	3.07	3.82	4.74	5.87
24	1.27	1.61	2.03	2.56	3.23	4.05	5.07	6.34
25	1.28	1.64	2.09	2.67	3.39	4.29	5.43	6.85
26	1.30	1.67	2.16	2.77	3.56	4.55	5.81	7.40
27	1.31	1.71	2.22	2.88	3.73	4.82	6.21	7.99
28	1.32	1.74	2.29	3.00	3.92	5.11	6.65	8.63
29	1.33	1.78	2.36	3.12	4.12	5.42	7.11	9.32
30	1.35	1.81	2.43	3.24	4.32	5.74	7.61	10.06

Table 1

CHAPTER FIFTEEN

HOLDING ON TO WHAT YOU'VE EARNED!

To predict the behavior of ordinary people in advance, you only have to assume that they will always try to escape a disagreeable situation with the smallest possible expenditure of intelligence.

– Nietzsche

BY APPLYING THE rules, strategies, and techniques, mentioned throughout this book, and with the aid of Almighty God, you will, if you have not already, started to acquire a certain level of wealth. You have worked hard to gain what you have; you have played by the rules, and made certain sacrifices to get where you are currently, and you deserve to enjoy the benefits in your retirement. Therefore, the last thing you want to see happen is to lose some or all of your wealth due to ignorance of what realistically can happen in our litigious society. You need to be taking the necessary steps to prevent or reduce your liability exposure whenever possible.

The subject of protecting your assets is a "meaty" subject, and a whole volume of books has been dedicated to this subject. Therefore, the purpose of this chapter is simply to provide you with an overview to describe certain steps you can take to reduce your risk to the lowest common denominator.

Due to forces beyond our control, such as annual inflation "eating" away at the purchasing power of every dollar we earn, we are forced to invest surplus dollars in order to earn an annual rate of return that is equal to or greater than the level of inflation. Unfortunately, we no longer have the luxury of keeping money under our mattress or a safety deposit box. So when we invest our money there is always going to be risk involved. Knowledge, however, helps to dispel fear, and it also helps us to avoid mistakes. Fear is often described as an acronym F.E.A.R., which stands for False Evidence Appearing Real!

RISK VS. REWARD

Every person has a different capacity and tolerance for risk, and there is a difference between the two. We know that risk capacity is a practical measure controlled by assets, sources of retirement income, and what we spend. If there is no gap between what we expect to spend and the amount we expect to receive from Social Security and pensions, then our risk capacity is high because income coming in is about equal to monies going out. If on the other hand, there is a wide gap where income is less than what we will be spending in retirement, then our capacity to take investment risk is low because we can't afford to lose.

Risk tolerance is different. It is more psychological, and has to do with our emotional ability to manage losses without panic selling. So when we allocate our investments into different types of assets, we need to consider our risk capacity as well as our risk tolerance. The point of all this is to simply state that there is a definite relationship between risk and reward. The more risk we are willing to take, rationally speaking, the greater the potential reward or return on investment. The reverse, of course, is also true. The less risk we take, the lower the return on the investment.

As you can see, our financial system, in a way, forces us to take certain risks to offset inflation, that put our investments in potential danger, and sometimes our entire accumulated assets can be exposed to loss under certain circumstances. Therefore, for the rest of this chapter, I am going to cover a number of ways you can reduce your risk, either through foreknowledge, or completing steps that can help reduce your risk to a lower, more acceptable level. It is pointless to work hard in accumulating assets for your retirement if you do not take proper action to protect them. Keep in mind, however, that you only need to take action on those issues that may apply to you.

THE UNIFORM FRAUDULENT TRANSFER ACT (UFTA)

This Act, adopted by most states, says that a party may not gratuitously transfer property to another (including transfer into a co-tenancy) if his or her intent in doing so is to defraud creditors. The UFTA states that such an intent is presumed if the transfer thereby renders the party insolvent, thus denying a creditor an opportunity to seize the debtor's assets.

The lesson to be learned by UFTA is that pre-planning for asset protection is very important. Please note that by bringing this Act to your attention, it is being done so from the position that all the readers of this book are honest, law abiding citizens who do not want to take advantage of anyone. However, if you happen to have a high risk occupation, or own a business with the potential for liability, then you should take steps to protect your home and family from factors that are beyond your ability to solve. One such action would be to transfer ownership of your home into your spouse's name, but it must be done well in advance of any law-suit being filed against you. Also, not to scare you, but if you injure someone, the claim is usually divided into three parts: economic damages, non-economic damages, and sometimes punitive damages. Claims can be awarded into the millions of dollars, depending on the circumstances involved. Personal insurance, in such circumstances, may not be enough to cover all the costs.

Unfortunately, there are too many lawyers who will sue on a contingency basis, whereby the plaintiff pays nothing out-of-pocket, with the lawyer paying for his client's legal fees out of his own pocket, in order to receive about a third of the proceeds if he wins the case. The defendant, on the other hand, pays all his own legal expenses, even if he is found innocent of all charges.

Meanwhile, the plaintiff walks away cost free. In this regard, The United States legal system is different than other western developed nations such as Canada, Australia, New Zealand, and Great Britain, where the plaintiff pays for both sides if he loses the case. So it is easy to see why so many frivolous law-suits are filed, and until we get tort reform, we must live with this reality.

FEDERAL AND STATE EXEMPTION LAWS

A federal law known as the Employee Retirement Income Security Act (1974), referred to as E.R.I.S.A., was formed and designed to protect employee pension funds from creditor seizures. This law has also been upheld by the U.S. Supreme Court. To qualify under ERISA, the pension plan must: 1) be subject to ERISA rules, 2) be tax qualified under ERISA rules, and 3) must contain an anti-alienation provision. Most private pension plans meet these requirements. It should be mentioned, however, that a pension plan covering just the owner and his spouse, is not considered under ERISA plans. Also, ERISA does not protect against IRS tax liens, alimony, child support payments, non-qualified plans, self-employed retirement plans (SEPs), or individual retirement plans (IRAs). The last three, however, are covered in some state statutes (see below). Notice also that many employees role over their 401K pension plans into an IRA when they change jobs in order to gain more flexibility in investment choices. This could be a problem if the state in which they reside has no provisions for protecting IRA funds, like California, thus exposing the funds to creditor claims. This would not be the case if the funds stayed inside a 401K plan. So always check your state law before making such decisions.

SOCIAL SECURITY AND OTHER FEDERAL GOVERNMENT BENEFITS

If a creditor sues you and wins a judgment, it can obtain a court order to garnish your bank account to collect the judgment debt owed. However, Social Security checks that are directly deposited into your bank account by the government are fully protected under U.S. Treasury rules. If, on the other hand, the SS funds are not directly deposited, or if you transfer the SS funds to another account, then the SS funds are available for creditor seizure. This rule also applies to: Supplemental Security Income, Veteran Benefits, Federal Railroad Retirement, Unemployment and Sickness Funds, the Civil Service Retirement System, and the Federal Employee Retirement System.

INDIVIDUAL RETIREMENT PLANS (IRAs)

IRAs, as mentioned, are not protected from creditors under federal laws, which is a pity because millions of Americans have more than $8 trillion invested in such plans for their well deserved retirement. However, a number of states such as Arizona, Alaska, Florida, Idaho, Missouri, Ohio, North Carolina, and Texas, do have laws that protect IRA retirement monies. Therefore, I suggest to all readers to check your own state laws to determine whether your IRA funds are protected from creditor claims. Meanwhile, because I happen to live in Arizona, I will simply mention some highlights of the Arizona model in order to provide a flavor of how some states operate regarding this subject of IRA protection. Under Arizona statute 33-1126, it states that "Money or other assets payable to participants or beneficiaries in various retirement plans are exempt from all claims of creditors of the beneficiary or the participant." The coverage applies to 401K pension plans, and IRA plans, that fall under IRS code 408. This law also applies to life insurance policies, health and disability policies, annuities, Section 529 college savings plans, child support receipts, and the earnings of minor children of debtors and so on. Unpaid child support and IRS tax liens are not protected in an IRA under Arizona law.

If you would like to know more about the $26 trillion in retirement plans, including Employer Defined Benefit Plans ($7+trillion), Private Sector Defined Benefit Plans ($3+ trillion), Government Defined Benefit Plans ($5+ trillion), IRAs ($8+ trillion), and Annuity Reserves ($2+ trillion), you will find useful information at the Investment Company Institute's website: www.ici.org.

HOMESTEAD PROTECTION

Homestead protection acts vary from state to state with regard to laws that protect a person's home from creditor seizure, and therefore you should verify your own state law. In Florida, for instance, 100% of the equity you have in your home, irrespective of value, is fully protected from creditor claims. In Arizona, the first $150,000.00 of equity is protected from creditor claims. For instance, if you live in a home with a value of $200,000.00, and you owe a mortgage of $75,000.00, then a creditor could not force the sale of your home. Arizona also protects life insurance, annuities, and IRAs, as mentioned.

OTHER PROTECTED INCOME SOURCES

Generally speaking, the following sources of family income are protected from creditor claims:

- Unemployment funds
- Worker Compensation payments
- 75% of wage garnishments

TITLING REAL ESTATE OWNERSHIP:

Holding title to real estate varies across the country, and therefore I will only be discussing the community property states that include: California, Washington, Idaho, Arizona, Nevada, New Mexico, Texas, Wisconsin, and Louisiana. In any event, it is always advisable to check your own state law before closing a real estate transaction. Unfortunately, many home buyers do not, nor do they seek legal counsel.

The five most popular ways to take title to real estate, and the pros and cons involved are as follows:

Sole Ownership

This method of taking title is also known as ownership in severalty, and is used by single men and women who hold title in their own name. This form of titling is also available to married couples, but if this method is used, then the spouse is usually asked to sign a quit claim deed, which voids any ownership rights in the property. There is usually some special purpose involved when a married person uses this form of title taking because there are no special tax advantages, and upon death the property is subject to probate before sale proceeds can be disbursed.

Tenants in Common

This form of title ownership is used when two or more people take ownership, especially if they are not married. Investors often use this method whereby if two people are involved, then the deed can determine each owner's proportional percentage of ownership. It could be 50/50, or 60/40, whatever the parties decide. Each party can then sell their ownership percentage, or deed it in their Will to any third-party they choose. This method of titling is also popular in second marriages whereby each owner can Will their ownership portion to children from their first marriage. However, some disadvantages are involved with this type of ownership. For instance, a sale is subject to probate costs and delays. Also, an owner can end up owning the property with a complete stranger. Partition actions can also be taken to force the sale of the property by a partner who wishes to sell when the other does not.

Joint Tenancy with Rights of Survivorship

Using this method of titling, both parties take ownership at the same time, and own an equal share in the property. The surviving owner ends up owning the entire property. This is a very popular form of ownership between a man and his wife, and is also called tenancy by the entireties. When one party dies, their Will has no bearing on the equitable title of the property, as it has already been pre-pledged in the title. One of the main advantages of this form of title is that it avoids probate and all the costs and delays it entails. One disadvantage is that one of the owners can give or sell their interest in the property without permission from the other party. If there are only two joint tenants, then the title would change under such circumstances to a tenancy in common.

TRUSTS

A good way to take title to real property is by placing it into a trust, which is of two types – an inter vivos or testamentary. Inter vivos trusts, or living trusts, may be revocable or irrevocable. The testamentary trust is created by the decedent's Will and becomes irrevocable upon the decedent's death.

Revocable Trusts:

Under normal circumstances, revocable living trusts are a better way to take title than the other methods mentioned, because they avoid costly probate, and other than the start-up costs, which cost about $1,500.00 give or take, and the transferring of the title into the trust, there are no real disadvantages. If you decide to set-up a revocable trust, you can transfer other assets into it such as stocks, bonds, mutual funds, annuities, personal property, and automobiles etc. You can still buy, sell and transfer assets in the ordinary course. Also, if the trustor/trustee is you, for instance, and you become disabled, incompetent, or die, then the named successor trustee takes over the management of the trust in accordance with your wishes as stated in the trust. A Trust also maintains privacy, whereas a Will is available to the general public. Revocable trusts, however, are subject to creditor liens, whereas an irrevocable trust is not.

Irrevocable Trusts

An irrevocable trust provides protection of your assets against creditor claims, because you are in fact giving up control of the trust to someone else. Therefore, claims against you cannot be applied against an irrevocable trust arrangement. Such a trust can be used to provide security for relatives who do not have the inclination or the financial acumen to manage a trust, and this prevents the possibility of irresponsible or incompetent decisions that could put assets in peril. Also, if you have an occupation, such as a doctor, surgeon, or even a real estate broker, where you are constantly being exposed to high risks of potential liability, or you own a business that has liability potential, then you may consider setting up two trusts, one revocable, and the other irrevocable. Because the irrevocable trust is immune from creditor claims, you may wish to place your home inside such a trust, in order to protect your wife and family from possible eviction if you lose a law-suit. Due to the fact that you give up your rights to all assets placed inside the trust when you sign off, you need to think the matter through carefully, and consult with a lawyer, before proceeding.

BUSINESS ENTITIES

Establishing a business entity for your business, as mentioned in chapters nine and ten, will not only provide you with greater taxable deductions, and accelerate your wealth holding value, but a business entity can also be a great method for protecting you against liability. While the entity helps shield you from liability, you can also add insurance protection to further protect yourself.

INSURANCE PROTECTION

Even if you never leave your home, you are at risk, because life is full of risk. Yes, you can reduce some risk by locking your doors, driving within speed limits, and taking steps to transfer your risk to a third-party, for a fee. We call it insurance protection, and in America we have created a multi-billion dollar industry built on accepting the risks of others. There are numerous insurance policies available, and if you are not careful you can become "insurance poor," by purchasing too much unnecessary insurance protection. Some insurance, however, is prudent, in order to protect you against perils that could bankrupt you in some instances. What I find most interesting, is the fact that we all live in the safest country in the world, but we also own the greatest number of insurance policies to protect ourselves. It somehow seems so odd to me.

So, if you want to create an insurance program to protect your family, and a business you may own, you need to tailor it to your needs taking economics into consideration. But before you begin, you should obtain clear answers to the following:

1. What types of insurance do I need?
2. How much coverage do I need?
3. What is the cost?

Some Insurance Tips:

1. Know the current value of what you are insuring. If, for instance, your home is worth $250,000.00, and the land (which cannot burn or be destroyed) is valued at

$100,000.00, then consider insuring the building for a $150,000.00 replacement cost, and save money.

2. When searching for automobile insurance, be sure to have enough liability coverage. In many states, the minimum liability insurance amounts are very low. In Arizona, for instance, the minimum is only $15,000.00 per person and $30,000.00 per accident for liability coverage in an accident. Property damage is limited to $10,000.00. This may be OK if you have no assets, but if you own property or a business that you need to protect, then you may want to consider obtaining an umbrella policy that will protect you for a much larger amount in the event you injure someone. Otherwise, you are on the hook for any claim amount above your insurance limit.

3. Do a search to ensure you are getting all the insurance discounts available for such things as a good driving record, installing smoke and alarm systems, or having an insurance gizmo installed in your car by the insurance company to monitor your driving habits.

4. Choose the highest deductibles in order to reduce your premium cost.

5. Shop three different insurers to get the best quotes before purchasing.

6. Buy all your insurance from one source to obtain packaged discounts.

7. Work with an independent insurance broker who has access to multiple insurance companies to provide you the best insurance program.

SOME FINAL THOUGHTS

I have often been amazed over the years by the number of people I have known, who take out insurance to protect their own lives, their family, their health, disability, homes, automobiles, boats, and even identity theft insurance, all of which come at a considerable cost. However, these same people fail to take advantage of the one insurance policy that guarantees them all an eternal life after this limited, mortal life ends, and the policy comes with no premium payment whatsoever! It is absolutely free, yet they refuse to accept it. So, don't you think it strange, that people will bundle themselves up with all types of insurance to protect themselves against unknowns in this world, but won't take any steps to insure themselves against their uncertainties in the next world? Yet, a good reading of the Bible clearly tells us that we can enjoy a 100% guaranty of eternal life after this one, by simply accepting Jesus Christ as Lord and Savior. Imagine a future life where we will not have to worry about financial planning for our retirement, or have any concerns about our health, or growing old and decrepit. It is all possible, provided we believe in Jesus! We all know that this life is temporary, and one of my favorite Christian authors summed up our life on earth very clearly when he once said, "All that is not eternal, is eternally useless!"

As I look back on my life, and realize how quickly time has turned me from a young to an older man, I praise God for the help He gave me along the way. I now live a comfortable retirement, but I also see many people in my peer group that are struggling with finances, and worrying about the future. I don't want this to happen to you, and that is why I have written this book. I sincerely hope that God is pleased with the end product, which is designed to provide not only hope for you, but clear and simple steps that can be taken to ensure that you too have a good, dignified retirement to look forward to.

Finally, I must stress one other subject that has nothing to do with this book, but is important nonetheless. I am referring to the need for us all to maintain the very best health that we can, especially as we get older. None of us expects to live forever, but we also want to avoid crawling towards the finishing line if we can avoid it. Is there any point in working all our lives for a great retirement, while at the same time neglecting our health? Spending our retirement visiting doctors and hospitals sometimes cannot be avoided, but if there is anything within our power to prevent such an experience, we should be doing it now. So why not go out in style by maintaining good body weight, eating only nutritional healthy foods, exercising both your mind and your body, reducing stress wherever possible, and finally enjoying a good conscience clear night's sleep to reinvigorate ourselves for the challenges of tomorrow? God bless and God speed!

Have thine own way, Lord, have thine own way.
Thou art the potter, I am the clay.
Mold me and make me, after thy will,
While I am waiting, yielded and still!

THE END

Mesa, Arizona

EXHIBIT "A"

SELF-EMPLOYMENT TEST

BEFORE YOU LAUNCH into starting or buying your own business or franchise, you need to clearly understand yourself and what it is you are trying to accomplish, and why. You may be motivated by many reasons, some good and some not so good, but whatever drives you has to match the type of personal profile that is needed to succeed in business. So before you do anything, I advise you take the test below. If you score 25 points or more, you should proceed. If not, then you need to work on your weaknesses first, and then entertain self-employment. For each "yes," answer, give yourself one point. A "no" counts as zero points, and you get a half-point for every question mark.

1. Do you enjoy good physical and emotional health? _____

2. Will your spouse, children or friend help in the Business? _____

3. Are you a good numbers and money manager? _____

4. Do you have a strong work ethic? _____

5. Do your skills, education and experience
   fit the needs of your business plan? _____

6. Are you comfortable selling products or services, or both? _____

7. Do you possess good common sense? _____

8. Are you a self-starter or do you need to be pushed? _____

9. Are you OK managing risk without panic? _____

10. Can you multi-task?   _____

11. Do you like setting and accomplishing goals?   _____

12. Will you be willing to work long hours
    in the beginning?   _____

13. Do you thrive on competitive challenges?   _____

14. Are you comfortable leading others?   _____

15. Can you finish tasks on time?   _____

16. Would you characterize yourself as resourceful?   _____

17. Do you have will-power and discipline?   _____

18. Can you make good, solid business decisions quickly?   _____

19. Are you comfortable speaking in public?   _____

20. Can you stay reasonably organized under
    a heavy work-load?   _____

21. Are you afraid of failing?   _____

22. Are you afraid of succeeding?   _____

23. Are you intimidated by bankers, lawyers,
    accountants and IRS agents?   _____

24. Can you write clearly?   _____

25. Are you able to honestly assess your strengths
    and weaknesses?   _____

26. Can you bounce back from set-backs?   _____

27. Are you creative and curious?   _____

28. Could you hire or fire an employee
    in a professional manner?   _____

29. Do you have a good reputation for doing
    the right thing?   _____

30. Are you passionate about what you want
    to accomplish?

TOTAL   _____

EXHIBIT "B"

LIST OF (150) HOME-BASED BUSINESSES

Lawn services
Free Lance Writing
State Licensed Adult Care
Mobile Computer Training
Vending Machine Routes
Auto Buying Service
900 Number Services
Balloon and Gift Wrapping
Cleaning Services – Commercial
Jewelry Sales and Repair
Business Brokerage
Sales Training
Carpet Cleaning
Air Dust Cleaning
Image Consulting
Photo Business Cards
Mortgage Brokering
Aluminum Can Recycling
Condo and Vacation Rentals
Credit Repair Services
Radio Jingles
Telephone Message Service
Personal Buying Services
Direct Mail Coupons
Tutoring
Bus. Expense Reduction Service
Restaurant Food Delivery Service
House Sitting
Mortgage Auditing
Locksmith Services
Direct Mail Advertising

Music & Voice Training
Grant Writing
Network Marketing
Consulting
Mobile Windshield Repair
Utility Auditing
On-Site Vehicle Inspections
Cleaning Services – Residential
Billing Services
Mobile Auto Detailing
Real Estate Sales
Management Programs
Child Safety & Identification
College Scholarship Matching Service
Skin Care Products
Color Printing T-Shirts, Caps, Mugs
Mobile Roof Service
Travel Services
Apartment Rental Services
Signature & Handwriting Analysis
Wedding Planner
Telemarketing Services
Consignment Art Sales
Educational Guidance & Financial Aid
National Emergency Response System
Environmentally Safe Products
Expresso Carts and Machines
Pet Sitting
Cartoon Map Advertising
Referral Services
Mobile Power Car Washing

On-Site Health Screening

Employee Outplacement Service

Hotel and Travel Discount Club

Shoplifting Prevention Products

Importing and Exporting

Lawn Signs Rentals

Real Estate Appraisal

Yellow Page Consulting

Pizza Delivery

Tax Services

Success Books and Tape Sales

Mini Recording Studio

Personal Fitness Trainer

Limousine Service

Third-Part Loan Brokering

House Painting

Skip Tracing

Catalog Selling

Hairstyling

Yoga Trainer

Party Clown

Musician

Free Lance Copywriter

Interior Designer

Seller of Collectibles

Photographer

Baker

Caterer

Fundraiser

Life Coach

Publicist

Mystery Shopper

E-Bay On-Line Business

Home Inspector

Candle Making

Teach ESL (English 2nd Language)

Computer Training/Repair

Contractor

Insurance Broker

Maid Services

Medical Billing

Engraving & Personalized Gifts

On-Line Book Sales

Business Franchise Sales

Drone Aerial Photography

Home Delivery Services

Home Parties

Manufacturers Representative

Financial Consulting & Brokerage Service

Website Business using Drop Shipments

Trade and Barter Exchange

Mail Services

Business Snack Route

Used Car Buying, Restoring, Selling

Welcome Service Directory

Clothing Alterations

Uber Driving

Gift Baskets

Mobile Bill Board

Handy Man Services

Private Investigator

Chauffeur

Web Designer

Vintage Clothing Reseller

Dance Instructor

Music Trainer

Massage Therapist

Home Stager

Dog Groomer

Furniture Upgrader

Jam Maker

Florist

Landscape Designer

Professional Blogger

Glass Blower

Travel Planner

Amazon Distributor

Virtual Assistant

Senior Care Services

Business Coaching

Voice Trainer

Water Restoration Specialist

Pest Control Service

Pool Service Route & Repair

Moving Services

Medical Alert

Security Services

Property Management

EXHIBIT "C"

RESOURCES

BUSINESS PLANNING SOFTWARE:
www.BusinessPlanPro.com
www.LivePlan.com
www.SimplePlanning.Net
www.brs-inc.com
www.BusinessPowerTools.com
www.PlanMagic.com

BUDGET TRACKING:
www.budgettracker.com
www.geezeo.com
www.mint.com
www.Yodlee.com

Now that you have finished reading, *Managing Money Spiritually*, you may be interested in reading my first book, ***Your Last Chance to get it Right! (A journey from Darkness into Light)*** (2016). In this book I stress the importance of getting man's spirit right with God, because hundreds of millions of people are currently living in darkness, and live their lives without any purpose or meaning. We grow physically and mentally automatically, but we do not grow spiritually automatically. We need to develop the spiritual side of our nature to complete man's trinity of body, soul and spirit, just as God expresses Himself to all of us as a trinity – Father, Son and Holy Spirit. I heed the words of the great ancient Greek philosopher, Socrates, when he once said: "The unexamined life is not worth living." Our finite limited life-span does not give us much time to get an "A" stamped on our life experience, so time is of the essence. In the book of James 4:14, it says: "Why, you don't even know what will happen tomorrow. What is your life? You are a mist that appears for a little while and then vanishes."

If you are searching for answers to the true meaning for your life, you may wish to read my book, as I take you on a journey around the world (I have travelled around six continents and well over 100 countries),where I discuss the creation of the great empires, the great religions, and how man has devolved over the last 5,000 years in his relationship with God. This led to the bloodbath of the 20th century, where some 170 million casualties were caused by communism, fascism, and Nazism, all godless systems. By taking this journey, you will better understand why the world is in the mess it is in today, and what you and your family can do about it. Mary McCloud Benthune (1875 – 1955), summed up my sentiments when she once said: "Invest in the human soul, who knows, you may find a diamond in the rough!"

So, if you are already a Christian, you can use the contents in this book to appeal to both the heart and intellect of non-believers, or people who are struggling with the meaning of their life. I spent the first 30 years of my life living in darkness before I found the light of Jesus Christ as my Lord and Savior, and most Christians I know have a family member, neighbor, co-worker, friend, or even a stranger, that come into their lives searching for the right path to God. Imagine just for a moment that you are given the opportunity to be part of someone having their eternal soul saved through the redemptive blood of Jesus Christ! You may find my book a useful tool in fulfilling Matthew 28:19, the Evangelion Good News of Jesus Christ! May you be successful in this endeavor!

Your Last Chance to get it Right (A Journey from Darkness into Light), can be purchased either through Westbowpress.com, or by calling the author at 480-620-5857.

Thanks for reading, and may God bless you!

ABOUT THE AUTHOR

Alan W. Hayden has been involved in the financial industry for more than 40 years in various capacities. He has managed a number of consumer finance companies as well as steel manufacturing, where he was responsible for more than $400 million in steel building shipments per year, both domestically as well as numerous other countries. Alan has also appraised and sold more than 250 small to medium sized businesses in four western states. Now in retirement, Alan's only goal in writing this book is, with the help of God, to assist anyone who is struggling financially with no plan for their future retirement.

www.ingramcontent.com/pod-product-compliance
Lightning Source LLC
Chambersburg PA
CBHW060547200326
41521CB00007B/516